OUT HERE, WE SAY "MIZZOURA"

AN ANTHOLGY OF MIZZOURA POETRY

I0617829

Edited by Jason Ryberg with special guest
editor, Maryfrances Wagner, Missouri Poet
Laureate, 2021-2023

Spartan
Press

Spartan Press

Kansas City, MO

spartanpresskc.com

Spartan
Press

Copyright (c) Jason Ryberg, 2023

First Edition 1 3 5 7 9 10 8 6 4 2

ISBN: 978-1-958182-48-2

LCCN: 2023946980

Cover and title page images: Jon Lee Grafton

Author photos: Victoria Stempleman, Helen Hokanson, Mary Jane Edwards, Kevin Montgomery, Lauren Adams, Jon Ulasien, Casey Rearick, David Nall, Tom Gillaspie, Jennifer Velasco-Cafagña

Acknowledgments:

Special thanks to Maryfrances Wagner, The Missouri Arts Council, Mark McClane, Tony Hayden, The Osage Arts Community, and to the editors of the following publications where these poems were originally featured:

Jordan Stempleman: "Canned," "Delays," "Save On What You Are Looking For," and "Noted": *Doubled Over,* BlazeVOX [books], 2009. "Friday," "Thursday," and "Sunday": *No, Not Today,* Magic Helicopter Press, 2012 "Responsibility," "Agreed," and "For Us All": *Wallop,* Magic Helicopter Press, 20, **Marianne Kunkel:** "Sariah Complains Over Lunch": Bosque, "Abish Teaches Me to Run": Chicago Quarterly Review, "Salvation" and "Tent to Tent": *I-70 Review,* "The Carpool Year": *The Louisville Review,* "Naming Nephi's Wife": *Notre Dame Review,* "Keep Away": *Portland Review,* "Infertility": *Sprung Formal,* "I Guess" and "Reverence": *Rattle,* **Andrés Rodríguez: "**Cicadas," "The Nets," "Everything is Dark," "Letter from Midtown:" *Portal of Dreams,* Woodley Press, 2018, "Something That Remains," "Real Monsters:" *I-70 Review,* "North:" *Hubbub, Vol. 25,* "Mystic Jukebox:" *Zingara Poetry Review,* "Nighthawks," "Cat in the Rain:" *Flint Hills Review,* **Erin Adair-Hodges:** "My New Boss Has Been Thinking a Lot About Time:" *American Poetry Review,* "Black Thumb:" *The Adroit Review,* "Love Song as Iphigenia in a Teen Movie Asked to Prom as Part of a Prank," "My Best Friend's Abuser Takes Her to Court:" *Gulf Coast,* "Juvenilia:" *Green Mountains Review,* "Self-Portrait as Erinyes' Dating Profile," "Unmappable," "After Ever:" *Sewanee Review,* "Midlife/ Midwest:" *The Missouri Review,* **Sara Burge:** "Thirsty Girls:" *Atticus Review,* "Dear Toilet Scene," "I took the gun from my mother's hand:" *Prairie Schooner,* "The neighbor's drunk again:" *The American Journal of Poetry,* "The Failure of Smell-O-

Vision:" *Backwards City Review, Apocalypse Ranch*(C&R Press), "The Valley:" *River Styx 73, Apocalypse Ranch* (C&R Press, 2010), "Finally, I See My Mother:" *Apocalypse Ranch* (C&R Press, 2010), "My Husband and I Fight about Robots:" *Apocalypse Ranch* (C&R Press, 2010), "War Candy:" first appeared as "God of Chocolate, God of War" in *The Virginia Quarterly Review 85.3* and in *Apocalypse Ranch* (C&R Press 2010), **Marcus Cafagña**: "The Surveyor," "The Way He Breaks," "Modigliani: Venus Naturalis," "Mammography," "Something Faithful:" *The Broken World* (University of Illinois Press, 1996), "Suits," "Dogs," "Thorazine," "Brighton Prison," "Red Devils," "The Little Stars," "Gloomy Sunday," "The Other Side:" *Roman Fever* (Invisible Cities Press, 2001), "The Shoplifting:" *All the Rage in the Afterlife This Season* (Finishing Line Press, 2023), "After the Divorce:" *Abraxas*, **Justin Hamm:** "Smallest Crowd:" *I-70 Review*, "Suburbs, Small Town:" *River Styx*, "To a Folksinger:" *Sugar House Review*, "A Real Team Effort:" *New Poetry From the Midwest, 2014*, "Storm. Rural Missouri," "Farmers at their Morning Coffee:" *Escape into Life*, "Payphones in the Underworld:" *Pittsburgh Poetry Review*, "Rebekah, Just When:" *Nimrod International Journal*,"Federico Garcia Lorca Blues:" *The Inheritance: Poems and Photos*, "First Lesson in Vietnam:" *Heavy Feather Review*, **Mary Silwance:** "Of Being:" *Spank the Carp*, "What Will Be," "To Remember:" *Kingdoms in the Wild*, "Alongside:" *Well Versed*, "Monkey Mind:" *Sequestrum*, **Daniel Biegelson:** "(ך) :: What Have I to Say in My Wrong Tongue of What Will Come:" MAYDAY Magazine, "(ה) :: What Good Are Soft Syllables When Crows Sleep Like the Dead:" *Yalobusha Review*, (ʻ) :: Sand   Soda Ash   Limestone:" *Interim*.

TABLE OF CONTENTS

Introduction by Maryfrances Wagner

Sara Burge

Justin Hamm

Marianne Kunkel

Jordan Stempleman

John Dorsey

Erin Adair-Hodges

Mary Silwance

Marcus Cafagña

Daniel Biegelson

Andrés Rodríguez

Introduction

During my time as Missouri's 6th Poet Laureate, I have had two major goals. The first has been to put poetry into the hands and ears of Missourians who don't usually read poetry or go to poetry readings. My second has been to promote or highlight Missouri poets and publishers. Thanks to all of the poets (over 50) who have participated in some part of one of the projects, and thanks to Jason Ryberg of Spartan press and Ben Furnish of BkMk press for production.

As a result of Covid, I have not been able to have the usual Missouri Poet Laureate travel experience for public appearances. I've given readings, talks, and keynotes, taught workshops, judged contests, participated in book festivals, written poems, published a book, re-issued a new edition of *Red Silk,* been interviewed, and traveled around some parts of the state. I have done many events while sitting at my computer on Zoom, so I decided I wanted to create some projects that would help me fulfill my two primary goals and reach all regions of the state in a meaningful way.

The most significant thing I have learned so far as Poet Laureate is how many fine poets have lived or worked in Missouri for a large part of their lives. Through my projects, I have tried to represent all regions of the state, multiple styles, and diversity, but I know there are still many poets out there I don't know or was not able to contact to be involved in one of my projects. I know I haven't begun to represent all Missouri poets, but I'm not done yet, so there's more to come.

My first project was to create ten podcasts called The Literary State. Each of these is a ten to twenty-minute podcast with a Missouri poet. Poets answer two questions about the craft of poetry, give a writing prompt, and read two of their poems. The podcasts are available on Anchor, Spotify, and Apple, or those interested can google them and listen on their phones or computers. The goal is that people will listen to them in their car, while cooking dinner, sitting at a table with a pen in hand ready to write, or anywhere they usually listen to podcasts. I also hope that teachers and professors will share them with their students as the podcasts offer valuable information about writing.

My second major project was to create Tiny Books to highlight eighteen more Missouri poets. Each of these tiny books includes one poem. Each of those poets received a quantity of tiny books to distribute to people who do not usually read poetry—the grocer, waiter, doctor, dentist, mail deliverer, grass cutter, neighbor, etc. These tiny books have been incredibly popular, and I wish I had thousands more of them to distribute since there are over six million people in Missouri, and I wish everyone could have at least one of them. Some have reacted in wonderful ways of helping to spread them around for many to read, and I thank them for that.

The third project is this one—two anthologies. Ten poems from ten more Missouri poets in two anthologies published by Spartan press and in partnership with *I-70 Review*. Welcome to the words of ten Missouri poets in this anthology. Enjoy.

-Maryfrances Wagner, Missouri's 6th
Missouri Poet Laureate 2021-2023

OUT HERE, WE SAY "MIZZOURA"

I wish we were back in Missouri
Where the cottonwoods bend in the breeze
I wish we were back in Missouri
Hear the nightbirds singing in the trees
I wish we were back in Missouri
Ploughing land and praying for rain
Oh Jesse, take me home - let's start all over again

- Emmylou Harris, *Wish We Were Back in Missouri*

Sara Burge

Sara Burge is the author of *Apocalypse Ranch* (C&R Press), and her poetry has appeared in or is forthcoming from *Virginia Quarterly Review, The American Journal of Poetry, New South, Cimarron Review, Atticus Review, Prairie Schooner, The Los Angeles Review, River Styx,* and elsewhere. She teaches creative writing at Missouri State University where she serves as the Poetry Editor of *Moon City Review.*

Thirsty Girls

Our town has a two-year college
where locals can get an associate's degree
or rack up credits cheap before making our escape
because most of us can't afford the thought
of Ivy Leagues. I'm taking classes
with my best friend Dawn.
Our anthropology professor
is a young, bearded smokeshow
with a wife and baby and everyone knows
he's screwing the red head in the front row.
He talks down to most of us,
but we drink him in anyway.

It's Friday. Dawn and I skip PE
to drive around smoking skunky weed
in my rusted-out Sunbird. At the liquor store,
the short brunette works the counter so we can buy
wine coolers, splurge on a fifth of Canadian Mist
then head out to cruise Porter Wagoner Boulevard,
creep through Sonic to look for cute boys
lounging on their tailgates like mulleted leopards.
We ask one where he's from.
Koshkonong, he says.
Spits tobacco.

We decide to hit the rich side, up on the hill
where houses have big yards and more than one floor.

We round the first curve and there he is:
Professor Anthropology, mowing his lawn
shirtless. I let off the gas to take it slow,
admire the black shorts, messy ponytail,
every drop of sweat. We giggle low,
staring as if men like him are rare.

On the third pass, he notices us,
so we stare straight ahead and speed away
to find a dirt road where I can pull over,
wait the five seconds between turning off the engine
and the engine's stop,
then sit on the trunk, drink our bottles empty,
wonder why we didn't ask for more.

I took the gun from my mother's hand

and pointed it toward the woods like she told me to
I pointed it straight and never knew
what kind of gun it was
I aimed at the tree she told me to pretend
was a stranger at the door
was a man who wanted to take me into the woods
an ex who wanted me to take back my rejection of him
by making me take it back
I pointed the gun
my mother loaded before she told me to place
one hand under the butt for support
look down the snub nose
look at the erect sight
look down at my chosen assailant
see the porous bark
see the assault of textures
see the ripples of gray valleys
of unwanted advances
imagine the way you want him to die because
she was afraid for me
because she said I needed to know how to defend myself
stand and take aim
while she stood proudly behind because
I did everything she told me to and I did it correctly
it was her gun
from her nightstand

my mother placed a gun in my hand

my mother said

look into the woods and see

everything that could / might / will probably try

shoot and afterwards laugh

because if the first shot doesn't kill him

she said laugh

because that will scare him

make him pause

then shoot again shoot that motherfucker again aim

for heart or balls or head

where there's a mouth

so much talking at you

into you

because it's a privilege to take whatever he is giving

a city in his mouth

your steady hand

flatten that city

this gun this metal can reduce every inch of him

take aim

my mother said

find a tree in the woods

imagine what could happen

The neighbor's drunk again

and outside screaming at his dogs
who hunker behind slices of trees,
perpetually howling for love.

The neighbor's nice again
and says he likes our garden,
we're gardening geniuses.
He'd have a garden, too,
if not for his bad luck.

The neighbor's drunk again,
says he's calling the cops
because we're *loud fucking assholes.*
It's the Fourth of July. It's 9 pm.
His shadow staggers
in his backyard's dark.

The neighbor's dogs at 6 am,
tiny and yapping beneath
the bedroom window.
The neighbor yells for them to come in,
Comet! Apollo! Comet! Comet!

The neighbor's drunkenness
targets a man and his kid
bicycling down our street. Screams
he'll call the cops on them.

Screams he's a genius
and he knows, he knows.
The man flips him off and pedals,
laughing, all the way home.

The neighbor tells us he'll
get his gun. He's getting it right now.

The neighbor's shadow at our door again
to apologize because he was abused, he's
an alcoholic, he's an astronomy genius
he's sick he knows people.

An ambulance at the neighbor's again,
the third time this month.
Its siren splits the neighborhood.
Its lights like comets.

The Failure of Smell-O-Vision

*[T]he critics dismissed it as an unpleasant gimmick,
and it was never repeated in a feature-length film.*

-From the obituary of Mike Todd Jr., producer of the
1960 Smell-O-Vision film *Scent of a Mystery*.

Of course it never took off. Perfecting
the intricacies of coffee brewing, waves breaking,
a city bus rolling away in a puff of clutch and rubber.
Too much to overcome. Liz unrolling herself before Caesar,
unbathed barbarians hacking through the muck of blood
    and limbs,
great white vessels battling in space. A culture sick
from the formula for romantic comedies. And besides,
it's not all Julie Andrews on a mountain top. Torture, really,

all those scents embedded in memory, carefully locked away
and waiting for us to stumble across their triggers—
his favorite cologne, leaves burning the day she left,
the dinner cooking when mother, phone in hand,
slid mutely to the floor. The stink of war secreted
into theater seats. Too much best left in forgetfulness
lurches back. The victims of our private tragedies,
setting us up for the kiss, their arms around us in the dark.

Dear Toilet Scene,

Thank you for adding that glint of grit the movie needs.
An avant garde way to make the audience know
this movie is the real thing. That it's willing to go
to any corner, down any street. Unzip itself for relief.
The scene that shows us all how little the female lead
cares for veils of decorum. Panties pulled low—
women, in real life, never pee—her motivation flows
upon the water's still face, its mouth happy to receive.

Nothing advances plotlines like the destruction
of porcelain bowls by drunk-assed decisions
to shit with the door open. Nothing shows how far
this character's grown beyond sexist expectations
of having it all—job! babies! bouncily-quaffed hair!
Such authenticity. That toilet will make her a star.

Call and Response

I know nothing of chainsaws except
my grandmother's arm in a sling
because grandpa demanded
she keep a log steady. I learned
chainsaws were another thing to fear
from men's miscalculations.
He was a math teacher.
Just hold it.
I know what I'm doing.

Tonight, across the alley separating
our neighborhood's backyards,
a chainsaw rages
and its metallic song
is joined by a woman—
her voice almost matching
the chainsaw's rise and fall.
Her unhinged howling
tries so hard to follow correctly.
The woman

my grandmother knowing
her husband wanted more
than the best she could.
He wanted her pain
to be something
she could not own.

Even with her arm in a sling
she'd let me curl up on her lap,
her antibiotics and verses
of how she must keep the wound moist,
Praise Jesus, seeping into me.

The Valley, the Shadow

In the valley south of our house, sheltered
by a canopy of wood, Betsy was dying,
her calf, still inside her, already dead.
She stomped the earth bald, bellowing,
occasionally managed to push. Hooves appeared,
slick and still until sucked back.

My mother called the vet, even roused
my brother from a hangover to force labor.
In the valley, he found a rock to perch on,
smiling foggily at the situation, his life, perhaps,
until assigned a role. As the vet reached
deep inside of Betsy, my brother
held the calf 's feet, and they pulled
until it erupted in a wave of placenta and fluids—
gray, tongue-out, motionless.

And then the stench. Death had already
sunk into muscle and bone, and we all turned
and covered our mouths. My brother laughed,
vomited tequila or whiskey
as Betsy's uterus followed after its calf,
a great pink sac covered in red spots.
The vet pushed it back in, sewed Betsy shut.

The calf 's death could be traced back
through a chain of events—bad positioning,

the luck of being Betsy's first, the ignorance
of a woman whose husband had just left her.
But Betsy lived. Three years later,
my brother died just north of the valley,
his body blooming under the sun, delivered
to some other place. And if there were hands
that helped pull him through, I don't want to know.

Finally, I See My Mother

Seventeen,
I sit at the kitchen table with my mother,
my brother two weeks dead.
The television murmurs low in the living room,
a well-meaning friend reminding us
to brush our teeth, buy soft toilet paper.
It fills our house with familiar, shallow breaths.

We talk about what we need
from the store, an oil change overdue,
and I watch her cut her slab of meat
with slow strokes, her eyes down, and think,
Her son has died,
as if it just occurred to me. In that instant,
in that land of nothing before,
nothing to follow,
she ceases being my mother.
Her son is dead
and eating is tragic.

But silverware keeps clanking against plates.
The television keeps humming.
I want to offer comfort, tell her
I see her, not yet knowing
we will never fully recover.
Instead, I say a boy she's never met
wants to take me camping.

She doesn't care. She has nothing left for me
and I cannot blame her.
Her son is dead,
and I am seventeen.

My Husband and I Fight about Robots

We talk while we sit outside, smoke cigarettes in the moonlight
among night sounds, sticks cracking beneath the weight of
creatures unseen. Lately, he obsesses about robots.
Nanobots, precisely, and how I no longer need to refuse
having his head removed and frozen, that nanobots

will preserve us forever. Microscopic machines
whirring through our veins, eating cancer
and reprogramming blood to perfection.
Sounds parasitic to me. He's undeterred.
I blame the science book he reads in the bathroom—

The Singularity Is Near: When Humans Transcend Biology.
It claims that in our lifetime robots will stop our cells
from needing to replicate, ending the aging process
which the book classifies as another disease.
Not quite Rock 'em Sock 'em. Far enough from toys to
    frighten me.

More unnatural than decapitation and refrigeration
because we're supposed to get old and die.
This first fight ended in a truce when a white owl
descended from the woods to swoop up something small
    and brown-furred
from our yard, then flew to a tree branch to eat.

But the next time we venture outside, the robots reemerge.
He's read more of his book and throws "therapeutic cloning"
and "magnetic nanotags" into the battle. I retaliate with

"It's just not right." It's robots versus wooden spears.
He's decided we both need robots,

but I refuse to be tracked by the government or turned
into a Cyborg Soldier. Though he reassures me it won't be
     like that,
the cold digs in so we go inside where I watch a show
on the Man-Eating Lions of Africa.
Obsessed with my own primal terrors,

I cower on the couch while the narrator explains
that though most lions kill their prey before eating it,
some of the men who built the bridge across Kenya's
     Tsavo River in 1898
were eaten belly first, their eyes still open,
their brains trapped in full comprehension.

My husband says our son won't need a sphincter
because robots will eat everything we don't need. I say
At least you won't shit your pants when the Apocalypse comes.
We laugh, but the thought of one trillion ravenous nanobots
disturbs me. I'm frightened of "biocidal nanoparticles"

and "self-replicating nanotubes" and "nonbiological
     intelligence,"
partially because I don't understand those words, but mostly
it's the alien language, cacophonous absence of comfort.
He promises they won't eat us. They'll transform us.
But he alerts me to Gray Goo,

explains that with every leap forward in science comes its
dark half with a missing conscience and finger on the trigger.
If self-replicating nanobots invaded the planet, they would
eat every living thing in two days, and when that death is
    excreted, it will be gray.
Like steel. Like eyes reflecting from the tree line.

Once our plate's licked cleaned, the experiments of hunger
and evolution will end in a way those African lions and that
owl could appreciate, in a way every clawless, weaponless life
fears but never wants to imagine: bellies bared as victorious
teeth sink in, as something starts crawling just beneath the skin.

War Candy

*During WWII, the army consumed mass quantities of Mars company's
new M&M candies, as the chocolate shells could withstand any climate.*

Even the walking dead need sweets,
            candy their meat

with peanuts in caramel like maggots
            in amber. Harden them quick,

make them wicks that will light
            when deprived

of softness, silence, chocolate
            kisses for skinned and missing knees,

then hand over sugar, hand over home,
            lay hope on hopeless tongues.

Lifelong users,
            the dead-to-be are hungry.

Thank you businessman,
            thank you marketing genius

for our daily confection of cocoa,
            milky infection wriggling up

through grass and sand, ingested,
            subject to you, extruding within us

your newly improved design.
          Mars in the sky, Mars raising weapons

high above the bowed, bald heads,
          hands them salvation, a taste

of reason, the battlefield's heat
          never meeting treated chocolate

within its Kevlar shell,
          nested chocolate swelter marching across

open mouths, gobbling, melting,
          misused mouths, meat to topple,

morale to season,
          sugar to sweeten the meat.

The cities and suburbs and farms
          reach out for you, god of chocolate.

They offer their spawn to you, god of war.
          They open their lawns, their black,

worm-filled patches and overnight
          hatch flags, up through dirt march toy prizes

for new broods, mass-marketed and sized,
          perfectly fitted to a child's hand.

Justin Hamm

Justin Hamm's latest book is Drinking Guinness With the Dead: Poems 2007-2021. He is the author of three other full-length collections and two chapbooks in addition to a book of photographs. The founding editor of the museum of americana, Justin is also a 2022 Woody Guthrie Poet, a former Missouri Arts Council Featured Artist, and a former recipient of the Stanley Hanks Memorial Poetry Award. His written and visual works have appeared in *Nimrod, Southern Indiana Review, River Styx, The Midwest Quarterly, Sugar House Review,* and *New Poetry from the Midwest.* In 2019 Justin's poem "Goodbye, Sancho Panza" was studied by approximately 50,000 students worldwide as part of the World Scholar's Cup curriculum. Afterward he was flown to the WSC global round in Manila, Philippines, to deliver the event's keynote address.

The Smallest Crowd Ever to Attend
One of My Readings

was a lone grandmother in futuristic spectacles
who I worried had wandered in by mistake.
But she was a keen listener who sighed and placed
her hand to her chest at all the right moments.

God bless her.

In fact she was only a hair less enraptured
than the folks at this birthday party I once attended
where an admittedly gifted clown sat on a stool,
blinking his makeup-caked eyes and twisting
balloons into strange shapes from every kingdom,
phylum, genus, and species ever to feature
in a special on the Discovery Channel.

He was quite good. Even the adults were hopeless
with admiration, lifting their souvenirs to the light,
whistling, grinning and shaking their heads.
"He's an Artist," somebody's dad or uncle proclaimed,
and a murmur of agreement circled the room.
On a nearby table a coffee can overflowed with tips.

I'm not really bitter. I have always believed
jealousy can be a fine teacher, if we allow it.
From my distant corner, I nudged the cat away
with the toe of my shoe. Wiped the green
frosting from my mustache and began to write
everything down in my pocket notebook
under the heading "ideas for future readings."

Suburbs, Small Town Missouri,
Fifth Day of Protests

All quiet, except for the growl
of a lawnmower, a child
squealing now and then.
Chirping birds gathered
around backyard feeders.
The smell of butchered cow
burning on a charcoal grill.
A father and son walk
their guns, careful to obey
all the pertinent leash laws.
They carry plastic bags
to clean up any casings
dropped on neighbor's lawns.
An officer cruises through
on his daily safety patrol,
waving a free hand to power-
walking women pumping
their May-pale arms in unison.
In house after house the news
goes on and right back off.
The sunlight on the pavement
a bright white, so white
it is almost blinding.

To a Folksinger Just Arrived in the Midwest

Whisper salutations to your irises
and tie those strange ornaments
into your hair. Crawl from your
Volkswagen into the sweltering city
and pluck something evangelical
from your book of songs. Strum
your dulcimer and enunciate as if
to blow life back into fried chicken
or restore the red to petrified roses.
Give them mystery, ancestry.
Give them not too much skin.
Yours, never forget, is the music
of freight trains and holyghosts.
You need only the lungs to drown
out the daily discord, the ambulances,
the ring tones and the burglar alarms,
and the city will place its heart
on the steaming asphalt and ascend.

A Real Team Effort

And here you'd gone and told yourself
the morning couldn't possibly
get any worse, not after you realized
you'd left your jock strap swinging
from your bedroom doorknob, as you rushed
headlong into the purple prairie morning, late
again for the six am travel bus
and facing the prospect of a doubleheader
behind the dish without proper protection.

And that's when you see it: your mother's
souped-up Camaro comes peeling
into the high school parking lot, skids
to an action-movie stop in front of the bus
just as the driver jerks her into drive,
and now, incredibly, here is your old man
sprinting in desperation, a thief or a madman,
and there is something in his right hand,
something which he has tucked against his side
for protection, as if it were a football
or perhaps an enormous jewel of untold value.

There comes a pounding and the driver
cranks open the side door with impatience,
and then he has your jock, which he has just
received from your panting, sweat-slicked pops,
and he—the driver—is holding it out away
from himself as if it might be radioactive,
and now he's turning, handing it delicately to Coach,

whose face goes cruel with wind sprints
as he turns and passes it off to Klein the freshy,
cursed to the front seats for having ears
too sensitive for upperclassman conversation,
and Klein the freshy hands off to Castillo
the backup catcher who's gunning for your job,
and Castillo with a snicker gives it to Rosenthal,
and Rosenthal—God help him—holds the thing
a second too long and lifts it toward his nose.

Then Martin, Berringer. Then Jonesy and Little Nick.
And so it goes, every man's hands on your jock strap
until it reaches that SOB Looney, two seats up,
Looney who could reach right out and hand it
to you himself, save you that final humiliation,
but instead he passes it to the team manager
who is sitting in the seat directly in front of yours
because she's beautiful and because you planned it that way.
Now she turns and there it is, dangling between you,
frayed and a little off-white from two years of use.
Through the straps you can see her eyes, two dark
lakes where so many other sensitive boys have gone
and gotten themselves thoroughly and finally drowned.

You reach out to take what is yours, and you wonder:
is this what the old broken men think of when they stare
out their windows into empty backyards, swigging
their warm beers and sighing now and then?

Storm, Rural Missouri

Though the coming rain
announces itself by rustling
the distant corn,
the barns remain immutable
as weathered grey monks.
Without words, they pray
over the dog who sleeps
forever in his soil bed
beside the oranged relic
of a horse-drawn plow.
On rage the blood sugar wars.
The lust for nicotine continues.
The time-crumpled angels
pull on their Carhartt robes
and stand under wide awnings
as lightning unstitches the sky.
Here, every storm is forty nights
from stating the profound.

The Farmers at Their Morning Coffee

Hear what news passes their lips
between the slow, ginger sips
from steaming plastic cups
at the local Hardee's.

Hear the coded odes
to past courting prowess,
the ballads of Mesozoic-like fish
caught not by pole but old-fashioned
Lincoln-style wrestling.

Uniformed in shirtsleeves
and meshback feedcompany hats,
they tell of coon dogs
treeing iguanas, old flood stories
to rival Gilgamesh or the Bible.

They tell in hushed voices
of witchwives who watch and hear
from afar the truth of a man's heart.

Was another pitiful year
for the crops, says one.
Too wet to plant in the spring
and too dry to grow
in the summer, says another.
This one's circulatory piping
has clogged up again.

And now the cold, too, has returned.
They all agree it really is
the deep kind that settles
into earth and old bones alike.
Things are always just a little
bit worse than they were
this time yesterday morning.

Still, it must feel good to be
so old and alive on this frosty morning,
to drink such hot coffee
and perhaps pick over
a rubbery breakfast platter
while curing the literal truth
of its shameful lack of color
here at this table where all the seats
are filled for only God
knows how much longer.

Payphones in the Underworld

My best friend texts me
a picture of a letter my mother
sent him the year she died.
He had forgotten about it
and wants to know whether
I want it for myself?

But the power isn't so much
in the ownership.
It arises from the surprise
in seeing the long loops
of her letters unexpectedly,
how they seem to carry
the very sound of her voice.

The dead know these things.
At just the right moment
they leave off from doing
their secret dead doings
and find a payphone, fish around
for change deep in the pockets
of their burial suits.

The call comes through
and on this end I pass a Camaro
just like the one Mom
rose hell with when we were kids.
Or the V.C. Andrews novels
stacked at the community yard sale

resurrect in my mind the rhythm
of her breathing as she read
evenings by yellow lamplight
in our smoky trailer.

But it's no use calling them.
The dead almost never answer.
You only tie up the line
as they stand patiently by,
tapping bony fingers to skulls
and waiting for the ringing to stop
so they know for certain the need
for reminder has ripened.

Rebekah Just When the Drought Was Ending

But the best thing about Rebekah
was the way she floated always
beneath the scent of woodburn
and dusty Middle America,
her keen ranch-queen convictions
slicing deep and deeper into
the tiniest of daily miseries
with skepticism, demanding always
some proof before she'd concede
this life He pieced together for us
cell by cell with ever shakier Godfingers
contained even one malignancy.

Every bow-legged young bull rider,
every sunburnt farmer of someday
who stopped by to mend a fence
or just to offer genteel salutations
would see her backlit by sunset,
dream her into his own mother
and pray to the essence of the prairie
to do what old bones could not.

And it worked. She survived well enough
to give of herself four more seasons
among luckless kinfolk who every one
drank greedily the blood she squeezed
and felt the cracked lips of dry times less.
As long as there was some great need
into which she could empty herself

she could will the heart to continue
and none of the rules of dying applied.

But she must've seen that the new rain
wasn't baptismal or meant for her restoration.
When those stormclouds finally swelled
and burst into fat miracle drumbeats
she must've felt the change was coming on.
Why else open the windows so wide
with no thought for the evening chill?
Why else cut a hundred wildflowers
and arrange them into fiery clusters
but pour no water into their vases?

Federico Garcia Lorca Blues

These blues are lunar, blues of the moon
and the moonlight and the white spell
the moonlight casts on tree-stubbled hills.

They belong to Andalusia, yet I have seen them too
folk-dancing the streets of Chicago in a gale
and smelled them over the insulin bottle

my grandfather tilted every evening
before needling out the potion
that staved off the duke of all shadows.

These blues are blues that incubate in the eager
throats of scavenger birds latched
to the crumbling brick silos of the Ozarks.

But most of all, they are the blues of the four
varieties of human sleep--three of them defined,
the fourth still to be discovered.

First Lesson in Vietnam, 1987

It was how you stood on your trailer roof
all that sweltering Independence Day, caped
in a threadbare flag of our nation, encircled
by Budweiser empties, plates of burning incense.
It was how you stood there and also how,
lit from above by those colorful celebration
bombs, you made me believe in the myth
of the romantic savage. I had no idea then
what you'd tried to accomplish alone
in the toolshed with the extension cord,
nor how, in a few years, you'd be hauled in—
armed robbery, just days after the first
Gulf War broke out. I saw only your hair,
shoulder length, and your scarred torso
bare and bony, home to a tattooed menagerie
of fantasy creatures: elf, dragon, phoenix,
centaur, faerie, citizens of a land
to which you'd gladly defect. It was all that,
and it was how recklessly you lit
bottle rockets and fired them from your
hollowed-out walking stick. And it was how—
finally—when my father cupped his hands together
and shouted, Hey, Chuck, give it a rest, guy.
It's getting pretty late, you turned, delicate
as a dancer in the shimmering moonlight,
and offered him what little was left
of your mangled middle finger.

Marianne Kunkel

Marianne Kunkel is the author of *Hillary, Made Up* (Stephen F. Austin State University Press) and *The Laughing Game* (Finishing Line Press), as well as poems that have appeared in *The Missouri Review*, *The Notre Dame Review*, *Hayden's Ferry Review*, *Rattle*, and elsewhere. She is an Assistant Professor of English at Johnson County Community College. She holds an MFA in poetry from the University of Florida and a Ph.D. in English from the University of Nebraska-Lincoln. While earning her Ph.D. at the University of Nebraska-Lincoln, she was the managing editor of *Prairie Schooner* and the African Poetry Book Fund. She is the co-editor-in-chief of *Kansas City Voices* and *Kansas City Voices Youth*.

Sariah Complains Over Lunch

[My mother] also had complained against my father...saying: Behold
thou has led us forth from the land of our inheritance, and my sons
are no more, and we perish in the wilderness.

—1 Nephi 5:2, *The Book of Mormon*

This place blows, Sariah says too loudly
as she plops down in a chair
at a Thai restaurant I've told her
is my favorite. She points
to the speaker boxes above us
and rolls her eyes at harp music,
fans her frowning face
with frail hands so everyone knows
she's hot. When a young waiter
approaches, she quizzes him
about which curries do and don't
include cilantro. *I'm a super taster,*
she whines, *and that trash*
is like soap. We're telling
each other our flower garden woes
when her drunken noodle bowl
arrives; in the seconds it takes me
to split my wooden chopsticks she sips
and spits out the broth, one hand
raised and furiously snapping.
You're being so rude,
I blurt. *Please cut it out.*
She hisses *I've suffered too much*
to put up with surprise cayenne.
Before she catches our waiter's eye

I slam her hand to the table
and suddenly regret
ever admiring her sacrifices—
fleeing her Jerusalem home,
believing her husband's whispers
of a godly American continent,
sending back four sons
to fight a thief for a family heirloom.
I walked for years! she reminds me
and I snarl *Walking's not
so hard.* She says *I almost lost my boys!*
I shout *I can't get pregnant.*
She shouts *I'm best known
for bitching and moaning!*
And as our waiter rushes toward us,
a finger raised to his lips,
I take comfort in the few, flattering
details he's learned over time
about me—Mussaman curry junkie;
rarely needs refills; generous,
apologetic tipper.

Salvation

...and also Zoram took the eldest daughter of Ishmael to wife.
—1 Nephi, 16:7, *The Book of Mormon*

Myself, I'm the youngest of two daughters,
       which meant extra help in the bra

and first period departments. And I had
       all the comforts of a chapel wedding;

you, Zoram's wife, married your love
       in a tent in the wilderness.

Months before, your do-good father fell
       for a city prophet's prediction—

if your family followed his family
       out of a debauched Jerusalem,

God would be waiting on American soil
       to cleanse all heavy hearts.

Unlike you, when my father tried to move
       our big family from Alabama

to Georgia the spring I finished high school,
       I shouted *I'm staying put*

and he listened. In the Yellowhammer State
       I got hammered at every party

and, late one night, locked blitzed eyes
   with a surly, smoky punk rocker—

my eventual husband. What was Zoram like at first?
   While the prophet's shy sons

blushed beside your giggly sisters,
   were you mesmerized by gruff

confessions from that lone outsider—
   a thief's clerk the sons convinced

to flee the city and save his soul? Was there
   a night he squeezed your hand,

the wilderness brooding in moonlight,
   and muttered if you could love him

his stone-heart would float like an angel moth?
   For me, weeks after I Frenched

the punk rocker, he cut back on cigarettes,
   drugged on so many kisses.

Zoram's wife, we love the same bad-boy
   man, turned soft against our soft bodies.

Naming Nephi's Wife

And we did come to the land which we called Bountiful, because of its
much fruit and also wild honey…and we beheld a sea, which we
called Irreantum, which, being interpreted, is many waters.

—1 Nephi 17:5, *The Book of Mormon*

In the clearing: a place to pig out,
to build and name a ship.
It's time for the big sail
from Yemen to America. Nephi's wife
and Nephi—Brad Pitt body,
already melting rocks to make a hammer—
and I'm there, loud feminist.
I am free to squirt Reddi-wip
on my blueberries, honk goodbye
when I drive home at dusk.
I tell her it's not okay nobody knows
her name and she nods.
I say if she doesn't have one
we can fix that, and she nods.
Nephi's dad and brothers loosen
rocks from dirt, naming pale and cloudy
and nicked ones as they go.
They yell to me for mugs of water,
pointing and waving because
they've forgotten *Marianne.*
In the family tent, she
slathers honey on skinned pigeons
while I ask her sisters about
her birth certificate. All they want to do

is brag that she's a brilliant cook,

prays until she sweats,

is a breast milk machine,

is *something else,*

is how I realize this is power:

women too in awe to curse her name.

The Carpool Year

After Walter Rane's painting "They Did Treat Me with Much Harshness"

My wife with her tears and prayers, and also my children, did not soften the hearts of my brethren that they would loose me.
          —1 Nephi 18:19, *The Book of Mormon*

Kind Obispo, our neighbor
in Mérida, Yucatan, didn't buy a leather couch
for a four-year-old to violently flop on, yet there I was
each weekday morning, splayed on cushions
and crying so loudly I drowned out my mother's *Gracias.*
Obispo's daughter was my age; at our Mormon church
I admired her crisp-white tunic dress embroidered
with bright poppies bigger than my face. It made sense
to ride together to preschool, despite
my family just arriving from Nashville
and me not knowing any Spanish. *They talk in words
I can't think about,* I pleaded with my mother,
her hand on my back both love and a shove
prodding me next door. In an old photo, I'm the child
squatting on pavement, arms crossed,
as my classmates sing and march around me.
My hot tears on the cool, mahogany leather
didn't stop; I was still sobbing in October,
the end of the rainy season. Tears couldn't stop
my mother from latching Obispo's screen door behind her
to putter home just as, years later,
they wouldn't stop a mango-sized scar on my knee
after a car crash, my first boyfriend sexting
other girls, my parents' eventual divorce.

If not for a tube of artistic prints Mormon headquarters
mailed our Mérida chapel, I would've wailed
in the children's Sunday School too
but I understood paint: a woman
draped around a man's hips, his wrists
tied behind him to a ship's mast. As men with whips
lunge at him, a smirking man steers the ship
through gray, spitting waves. I guessed this story
got worse—maybe the storm is God warning
the men to let up—and in the woman's
weepy face I recognized someone done crying for help
but not done crying, someone skilled in the art
of expressing pain, hopelessness
not a reason for silence
but its own worthy refrain.

I Guess

Right after my parents' divorce,
people blurted the single question
they'd been dying to ask for years.
How'd they last a day?

Great sex, I was tempted to respond,
as if the thought of my sour mother
fondling my father's new rebellion,
a ponytail, wasn't joke enough.

I guess long ago they made
each other happy. What a sad
thing to have to guess. Once my mother
spoke of a nightmare in which
she walked to our front door;

in pitch dark, she twisted the knob
and a hand from outside twisted back.
I imagine if I shined a flashlight
on that intruder's face, I'd see
my ever-frustrated father.

Proximity without loving
was their creed, him plucking
a guitar in a room off the kitchen,
her clicking a noisy blender on,

so I couldn't believe it when my father said
Enough after all those nights
he laid in their waterbed, flirting
with escape but drifting nowhere.

Keep Away

It was a rare family vacation at the beach
and we hadn't brought surfboards, bucket
or shovel. My kid brother, who'd vowed
to his friends he'd come home with a tan,
dropped his t-shirt in the sand. I grabbed it.
Because I could, because it'd been ages
since our parents tried to intervene, I chucked
his shirt into the ocean. It bobbed like a fish
in the foam as he hollered *Hey, what the heck?*
When it washed up, I raced for it. I laughed
and threw the heavy, white shirt again.
We must've stumbled along the shore for half an hour
lunging for the giant spitwad, me winning.
I didn't consider that the shirt might vanish
and when it did, lost forever in far water,
I shrugged at my brother. Now he lives
in Madrid, where he's served on a Mormon mission
for more than a year. He sometimes writes
to say prayer conquers all, or that he loves me.
I miss him in waves that obscure his face.

Tent to Tent

The first woman winks and says
if marriage is a fire, lies are kindling—
her husband tells her she's a better kisser
than she is, and she tells him each goat he slays

is bigger than the last. The second woman's
older, more matter-of-fact. Forgiveness,
she says, is all that keeps a marriage strong.
I've been sent to knock on tents

by unhappy wives of a rival tribe.
God cursed the Lamanites, not us, they groaned,
so why do our husbands sleep around?
What tricks do those wicked wives know?

The third woman tells me
tireless love is tireless hands—
helping him up when he trips, tickling his chest
and down, pressing a cloth to his fevered head.

The fourth, a newlywed, answers cuddling.
The fifth giggles and points to a rug
and stubs of rope. I recall, years ago,
binding my husband's wrists without asking first

and when he said *Stop* I sank my face
into a pillow, too proud to apologize.
The sixth is hurrying to a lake for water
and shouts behind her that a good marriage

is like a drinking mug that's nicked
but never shatters. The seventh whispers
love is speaking softly when the other's napping.
The eighth woman mistakenly thinks

I'm asking for myself. She cups my cheek
in her palm and puffs out a sigh—
Poor girl, are you the type who doesn't need
anyone like you need to be right?

Infertility

Who is this baby I can't have,
a no-show, a slacker who keeps
slapping the snooze button?
The keys to where I am—
why won't it get off the sofa,
turn off the reality TV,
and look for them? I didn't
raise this baby to act this way.
I haven't gotten to raise her
at all. I've considered
she could be a *they* or *he*,
this baby too engrossed
in sending his 100th
text message to make
an appearance on my home
pregnancy test. He blows
gum into bubbles bigger
than my unfertilized eggs.
This baby has been wearing
the same gray bathrobe
for days stretching into months
and years. Where did it learn
such lazy habits? Not from
my husband, a Microsoft Excel whiz
who creates spreadsheets for bills,
his Fantasy Football league,
relatives' birthdays. Nor me,
who treats a phone call
from my mother as time

to scrub the bathtub
while chatting. Oh, that we
could be the petite
parents of a long-limbed baby,
or blond parents of a redhead,
who can't see
a resemblance and can still
laugh that life is good.

Abish Teaches Me to Run

...she ran forth from house to house, making it known unto the people.
—Alma 19:17, *The Book of Mormon*

She flings my old duffle bag in the park grass,
saying Leave it. I worry my sneakers,
jostled in the bag with a Gatorade, are now soggy.
Accessories are distractions, she says as we take off.
She's clearly one of those purist runners—
bare, calloused feet, flowing hair, who declares
stretching is as pointless as scented lotion.
Back in 90 B.C., she says, *when we wanted to run
we ran.* I picture her famous moment,
a story my father read me; a servant to a king
who became Christian and then fainted,
she sprinted through town shouting the good news
that the king was faith-struck. My father,
also a runner, said she was his favorite woman
in the holy book. I remember wondering why
my mother never ran. *Surrender all your thoughts
to the breeze,* she says. We round a corner
of the dirt path and though a cramp pricks my shin,
I feel strong. *Always look up and out,* she says
as we pass a tree puffy with blooms.
She plucks a yellow one and tucks it behind her ear.
My father said she watched the king fall,
and others in the court were so moved
they fainted beside him. She stayed upright
because, years before, her father had a vision
and she converted. Is this running coach a vision,

a willowy version of my father? *Inhale deeply,*
she says, *Open your mouth as if singing—*
advice that almost sounds like his. I expect
my father to appear and when he doesn't, I stare
at her, recognizing the peach-fuzzy calves,
the shaggy, gray bangs where my father is balding.
Next to me is my stepmother. This is our first
run together. The path ends and I slow to a shuffle,
hunching to unknot my back. She dashes
to the parking lot. *I must tell them about the gorgeous
geese on the lake,* she hollers behind her.
Each person she approaches looks surprised
yet nods and smiles. It's true—no one hates Abish.

Reverence

*My son…thou didst forsake the ministry, and did go over into the
land of Siron among the borders of the Lamanites, after the harlot Isabel.*
—Alma 39:3, *The Book of Mormon*

To runners, a trail is church.

I heard a pastor say church is its people.

My father prays when he sees a rare finch.

Every Sunday, my teenage nieces cuddle
in bed with their parents, watch TV,
call this *church*.

Lazy Sunday morning sex can feel sacred.

My husband and I watch *Mr. Rogers*
with a box of Kleenex.
Why is Mr. McFeely
so frenzied when Mr. Rogers
has the much harder job
preaching love?

My mother used to bake two
pillowy loaves of white bread
to take to Mormon church
for communion.

Men gingerly tore the loaves.

Everyone ate, licking their lips.
Some joked her bread was why
they came. Is bread church?

I first entered a Quaker chapel
and spun around and around,
never finding a pulpit.

Barely lifting her blouse
my mother quietly breastfed
my toddler brother in a pew
until an older man complained.
What was his definition of church?

In The Book of Mormon, only six women
have names, the rest lumped
into shapeless categories of wives,
mothers, queens or harlots.
The harlot Isabel must have been
fairly important to get a name,
though the 500-page book mentions her
only once.

Isabel, how many left their lives
to follow you?

A bored son in a long line of prophets
walked away from religious study
to sprawl underneath your bare body.

Your hair shimmering like stained glass,
your nipples as erect as steeples,
you were his teacher, in charge,
shushing him if he spoke.

Let church trail off and it sounds
like *shhhh*.

Jordan Stempleman

Jordan Stempleman is the author of nine books of poetry including *Cover Songs* (The Blue Turn) *Wallop*, and *No, Not Today* (Magic Helicopter Press). He edits *The Continental Review*, *Windfall Room*, and *Sprung Formal*, and runs the Common Sense Reading Series. Author website: https://www.jordanstempleman.com/

Canned

I am telling you, this isn't funny enough yet.
Knobs, you say, which is so funny. Knobs,
I say, which causes you to leave. In Phoenix
there are those fugas tardías that always meant
to hold out until the faraway devils all go grayish,
as just above the road, come back, as you insisted,
with new land to change our minds. No matter what,
there'll still be the warm-blooded and twice as many
that are cold-blooded. I will later, much later,
be identified as the one who liked to run the weather.
And you, even then, will never be undone or untaken.

Delays

If you can tell the difference between the sugar maple
and the leaves of the paperbark, there's no hope
we'll ever get along. When someone heavily refers
to a simple task as a mission, enormous amounts
of tension are released into the atmosphere,
and the fires are serious and restorative,
but we're still busy, so busy much of the time.
If the question is: snow or rain, I hope you'd say:
another. There are those stars that are so swollen
that they're losing it before our eyes.

Save on What You Are Looking For

I have been converted to accept
all forms of insulation. The netted
does she pass through, the fine hairs
at work with no instructions, and tiny
unambitious globes, so close to one another
they corner out the sun. Place a root cellar
on the list. Behind it, the brown bat at sizzle
in the skillet. I am over the island of cormorants'
drippy wings and the bull ride I promised
my god. We're pushing up ahead of the road
with our flown hearts to vent. Cotton you up
for the years. Item in, item out.

Noted

The funny thing is, I suspect I'll know,
in regards to this earth, how to one day
single out the moonlight. You're a mess!
You glow lame, and call it "the days of
the frozen may I have you." At the bottom
of the sea there are candles that make good
rooms of the bad. They are not orange.
They do not bleed. Changing the fixtures
means facing the dead insects in the dark.

Friday

I hope so much for the rabbling intentions
of our future, that they remain something we consider enough
to erect a separate guest house for, with sprinklers
that don't cost too much, don't cost anyone
too much, oh Christ, the country.
One dish falls and the others will not. I clean it up,
and then you clean it up, yet it's years later that we remember
who did what, finally pulling the mattress
all the way down the hall to sleep on anything we missed.
Perennial, bad romanticism. Well, it depends
on who calls who babe.
You wrapped the robot all wrong.
I'm starting to get infected again.

Thursday

When I took my eyes off you, it was only to see
how you got here. Sample: By and by. Sample:
I'll suffer to imagine how it's always been
the one sun you've looked after, and the other,
that I'm quite curious about.
There are atoms that are glorious
and have no say. I do the laundry, and what scares me
is the sodden grazing of one fabric
against the other.
I am owned by paper-thin flagrance
and sea level observers who make a living
by looking intense under a pink light. I am serious.
I pretend to be serious. You have to be serious.

Sunday

I picked a really yellow raincoat. Asked, how many times
will it work before I'm forced back in? Said, if I just lie here
long enough, I know it will get me, get through to me, and then,
beneath me, felt the awful tree, planted by no one I know,
cut through the mud right in through the floor.
The photographer said it was difficult to volunteer at the hospital,
the orphanage, the unemployment agency, but especially
at the desk for unclaimed items: The food was too spicy; Those
shoes hurt our feet; Enough of this memory or even that.
No one cares what happens to those moments, those things
that they don't like. We'll never love what's there alone.
Over time, something collects them, and if we help, this is joy.

Responsibility

I walked for hours last night.
The wind died and returned,
returned with other people walking,
not looking so wiped out.
My boots were worthless.
I stood on a lonely bridge over
a river and thought about throwing
those boots into the river.
There wasn't even one dog around.
The city felt completely wide open,
like an enormous exit taking care of all
of nothing at once.
I smiled down at the river like I always
smile at rivers.
I saw my wife looking back up at me
wearing too much eye makeup.
And now I don't know what to write,
which feels a lot like not knowing
what to say. What to say to my wife
when she looked up at me from the river
like someone who needed a hand.

Agreed

A mutual friend, who I don't trust
as much as you do, claimed
that God used to just blurt out—I love it,
love it. This was a time when landscapes
overlapped movements, well before
the proof of ass and bullets.
I admit I have trouble with connections.
It's kind of devastating to watch the dead
or even the willing move from where they were worshiping
the bump in the basement to make a family
with the pond whose only instructions are
to go brighter and clearer, you must.
Friendship is different.
You say, my grandmother was once a butcher.
I say, mine wasn't. And we know it'll be a struggle
to keep the other one happy, but okay.

For Us All

Over some thousands of years we developed holes,
dirt floors, awards, reprints, and prosecutions.
I killed my children in caves. I left my child's
pulled tooth on the marble counter.
The policemen smell of coffee, bladder of dog,
clenched homeowners outside the home.
If I possessed my problem, the way they possessed
my problem. In my mother's house there is god.
There is hearing about god. I am an athlete.
I understand the anteater. I demonstrate this
by drinking my drink through a straw in front
of a line of policemen. I close my eyes
as the anteater does. There are waterfalls.
There is an uncertainty about my rectum.
There's something sad. Where is the unsad wise
body? The strong unroached crying?
I will love people off.
What happened is I killed something in the swamp.
I thought of danger and I kicked something.
I thought of what should be drained, and I killed
one meat of peach, one unfinished child.
We are entirely out of our homes.
I don't do my chores anymore.
My blackhaired wife is a wild turkey now,
in this heavy branched tree with miles of feathers
tucked around her.
The policemen stand below, looking up,
feathers, so many feathers
come falling near their eyes.

They are fed and washed and suited.

They have the hands of newscasters.

One by one they run and return run and return.

In my car I want to know everything.

Outside my house I want to know everything.

There are no more homes.

The year I wanted gold I got gold.

I loved my human being. I employed my child

and my child got panicky.

The sound of rain was the sound of rain

on mushrooms.

Mothers ate brains. Fathers ate brains.

I tried not to show my brains to my child.

In my child's hotel room we could hear the policemen

hundreds of stories down on the street below.

I thought we'd die before we'd speak.

I took off my child's socks. I ate the toes.

I ate the aloneness. I ate idiotic death

regardless of death.

I tasted a factory town. I ate the factory town.

My blackhaired wife did not want to talk.

She began at what was natural.

She hovered above the policemen and began with what's crude.

All she ever remembered fell down.

People travelled anyway.

People ate from memory.

She unbuttoned her throat and more feathers came down.

I am merely a celebration that trembles.

Sometimes there is a human that measures me.

The rain begins to fall and we get rained on.

I get measured in the rain.

I sleep on my child in the rain. I set fires in the rain

in the cities for the policemen who watch.

John Dorsey

John Dorsey served as the first city Poet Laureate of Belle, Missouri from 2017-2019. His work has appeared in numerous books, magazines and anthologies since the early 1990's. He is the author of *Sundown at the Redneck Carnival*, Spartan Press, 2022, and may be reached at archerevans@yahoo.com.

East Coast/West Coast, in Southern Missouri

a high school girl with thick black glasses
& a baby bump barely concealed
by a second hand tupac t-shirt
stands on the front of her lawn
as a volunteer fireman
who didn't make it past the 9th grade
throws candy in her direction
with a pitching arm
that will never take him any further
than the next county over

a love story held together with tape
like the glasses
peeling in the summer sun

candy corn at her feet
like stray bullets
in a gang war
in a music video
that will last
the rest of her life

a baby under each arm
pacing east and west
a drive by that goes in circles
leading nowhere
always in a rivalry
with possibility

maybe the old owner of the shirt
fed the hungry
danced in an empty swimming pool
& swore there was music
that nobody else could hear

or maybe she actually saw
who killed tupac
& biggie both
& never said a word
because there was peace
in just letting things go
like the boy
who placed the shirt
over her shoulders
as she shivered
taking what she hadn't offered
to begin with

because when you wash out
the blood stains
all you're left with is
your own heartbreak

standing on your front lawn
wearing someone else's dream
shrunken down so many times
with wrinkles
that you can never
quite smooth out
until you're almost invisible
with a snow cone melting

down your arm
in the sun
bleeding red white & blue
as a single sock
fresh out of the dryer
sticks to your belly
& that's the best part
of your day.

Passing Through Leadwood

for daniel crocker

just off the ferlin husky highway
i think what would richard hugo
say about this town
that you haven't screamed
in your sleep
a thousand times before

fueled by wonder bread & poison
sad songs about tradition & empty storefronts
the ghosts that go away quietly
because they know
that they won't be missed

the buildings that crumble
& just slip away
from their foundations

the houses that look normal
the regret that is bought
& paid for
in generations of blood

where the sky is a rusted satellite dish
a dirty diaper on the sidewalk
next to the high school

you & icarus are famous here
like ferlin husky on the wings of a dove

traveling through the body like cancer

on its way to somewhere else

some far away land

where there is nothing to do
but sing.

The Footlights of Hannibal, Missouri

went out with the ziegfeld follies
here rivers baptize their dead
running up against
the tattered edges of trailer parks
on the less than posh side of town
where a children's theater
once told the story of mark twain
at every matinee
as portrayed by the ghost of a 12 year boy
whose voice never got to crack
like a black walnut
under the weight of work boots
in the factory town
this once was
without even a hint of peach fuzz
along his upper lip
here where rumor has it
old samuel clemens was a creature of habit
who liked his sandwiches
with the crusts cut off
& the dead
kept in their place.

Poem for Edward Gehlert

there are birds singing outside my window
they don't know that there were nights
when there were no books in your room

mine either

they don't know that there were nights
when your heart was shaped
like a broken dinner plate

because some traditions
have dark designs

forget their values

nobody ever told us
that there are easier ways
to die inside

nobody ever said
that the dead
came back as birds

that felt lucky
to be able
to sing
at all.

Easy on the Eyes

there is nothing nice
to look at here
except fried eggs
black coffee
& a picture
of a teenage beauty queen
standing next to a prized hog

both of them
headed to the processing plant
one to pump out babies
like factory widgets
& one to become breakfast meat

both of them smiling
wearing blue ribbons
around their necks
putting on a brave face
for the camera
etched in grease splatter
for all eternity

their expressions
just hanging there
like a noose.

Tammy Talks Tough

tammy storms into the pool hall
screaming about how
she's been driving around
on one lug nut

saying that she knows
that her ex-boyfriend
is trying to kill her

she squeezes her fists
wrapping her dreams
around a warm bottle of stag
& the cool silence of nights like these

saying that he used to make her feel tender
every time they slow danced
to johnny ace on the jukebox
she pledged her love

but now the only song
that touched her lips
was dead man's curve

but that that was alright
he would get his

she said that her current boyfriend pickle
had fixed her car himself
& that he knew his way around a lug nut
and all of the tattered edges
of her heart.

.

Laddonia, Missouri, Population 502

one near empty roadhouse
just up the highway
from the mexico border
the gay black bartender
who never got out after high school
jokes around with the same guys
who threatened to string him up
in a tree
on prom night
his past is a closet
covered up with cornstalks
& nervous laughter

a headless teddy bear
offers a glimpse into history
but its mouth is a ghost
that can no longer share its story

the silver boom never brought
many people here
now it's just empty lots
filled with abandoned fishing boats
& covered over with grass
& the bones of flowers
that die every summer
only to be reborn
coming up through the cracks
in the cement
surrounded by broken beer bottles

from another season
that passed so long ago
that it feels like another lifetime
where not much has really changed.

The History of Rivers

a car with one headlight
bobs and weaves its way through the mud
looking for a pair of missing glasses
what good are they anyway
we can never see where we're going
only where we've been
floods of emotion like this
are only supposed to happen once a century
but we can't see our way past the rocks
everything only seems to come into focus
after we get out of the water
& raise a glass to the spirits
resting in capsized riverboats
that you'll never find squinting in the sunlight
listening to the words of that lonesome whippoorwill
singing some far-fetched river song.

A Collect Call to Coyotes

the afternoon sky is thick
with ladybugs & bees
somewhere in my past
a girl fries eggs
smiling naked as a jaybird
covered in dry paint
from a window
across the courtyard
now it is 6 am
& deep in middle age
her name comes back to me
i am alone here
i cannot teach a young dog
how to howl
or to mask its joy
running along an invisible river
where the grass
can still lead you home
where time
still does
what you tell it to.

13 Ways of Pan Frying an Armadillo

crazy mark says you'll need a good skillet
& the right amount of spices

also it's better if the moon is full
& rain is tapping against
your kitchen window just so

after all we're not savages here

but anything tastes better with hot sauce
that's just a fact

if the poor creature struggled
before finding true love
& dying peacefully in the tall grass
that just adds to the flavor

when i mention the risk of leprosy
he says you can fry
almost anything out
even the scent of death
blowing in the missouri wind.

Erin Adair-Hodges

Erin Adair-Hodges is the author of *Let's All Die Happy,* winner of the Agnes Lynch Starrett Poetry Prize, and *Every Form of Ruin,* both from the Pitt Poetry Series. Recipient of the Allen Tate Prize and the Loraine Williams Poetry Prize, her work has been featured in *American Poetry Review, Gulf Coast, Kenyon Review, PBS NewsHour, Ploughshares, Sewanee Review,* and more. She has received fellowships and scholarships from the Adirondack Center for Writing, Bread Loaf Writers Conference, Sewanee Writers Conference, and Vermont Studio Center. Born and raised in the Rio Grande Valley of New Mexico, she now lives with her family in Kansas City, Missouri, and works as a fiction acquisitions editor.

My New Boss Has Been Thinking a Lot About Time

Though he doesn't say exactly what this thinking
is about. He strokes his beard, a clock his face
has made, his right leg lifted to harass the chair,

his left on the floor, pulpited flamingo in tweed.
He tells me to *relax*, and maybe it's because
of the authoritative way he can grow hair

under his nose, but this command works
like a cauldroned incantation. I'm so relaxed
it's as if I have never, too, thought about time,

about the frenzied hours trying to settle
my son's dervishing, begging the languageless
to take my breast so we could be done

and I could get back to the work which would not
wait. I'm so relaxed I don't remember
how that son now tells me *seven was the worst year*

because that was the year I left to find a job,
how the time difference meant there were days
we could not talk at all. I pack the picture books

he has outgrown into cardboard boxes
I label for some future him's nostalgic need
for bears on quests, their orphaned hunts

for hats and homes and sleep. My mother never
saved such things—she thought I'd want to forget
those years. Sometimes what has happened never stops

happening. Even now—this windowed
conference room's smell of toner, the tea let out to stale—
our old disappointments dandruff the air,

a thought scrum of hurt. I am so relaxed, though,
I can finally be kind, so I cradle my boss, sing him
a lullaby until he burbles with joy. I could do anything

to his soft body. From a distance, this looks like mercy,
a freckled boy cradling the broken bird
his stone set loose from the sky. The woods outside

applaud. They have been waiting for the man in me
to come home. Another's blood the key.
The violence of time the door.

Black Thumb

The dogwood was threatening
to swallow the back garden's light,

so I borrowed a chainsaw and gas.
Its last berries a memory of red, the fruit

bitter, tiny angry mangos in the mouth
of its killer. Nights my son chooses his father

to read him into silence, I practice not loving
anything. Less like learning than remembering.

As a child, I studied how to be a child.
I was given a doll to care for

but could never remember its name.
I left her face down everywhere.

She had her father's eyes.
Each morning, she greeted me with a blankness

I chose to know as forgiveness.
There, there, I said and slapped her back.

There, there, I say to the tree trunk,
its pale O's of accusal.

From his bedroom window, my son eyes me
holding the humming saw.

What I look like to him is a memory
only he is born to bear.

Love Song as Iphigenia in a Teen Movie Asked to Prom as Part of a Prank

Mornings I wake to see what body the night has made,
praying the measuring tape to click out happiness's
three-spun locker code. Dear Diary. I scrawl my lamentations

in an alphabet of swirls, burn them at the altar
of straight hair, of the moon loving this blood away.
I was born and then I waited. Bounced around like an asterisk

in other peoples' stories. The pre-prom days an endless siege,
eyeing the beach for some boy to break through.
That bitch Helen, the school turned dogs for her

but still copying my math. My father hectors
the football field, whistle swinging round his neck
like a pendulum, counting down to something

he thinks I can't understand. What I should have known
I did not suspect. The invitation into my life. Into his, this boy,
gleaming from some god-river inside him. That he knew my name

meant happiness could learn it, too. My mother
brushing my hair, burnished like armor. Last-minute, the dress,
the clinging revelation. I leave my glasses off, scent my wrists

and neck. The pinned corsage of ecstatic amaranth
tasseling my breast like my heart's own blooming.
The crowd surrounds. They round their mouths in shock.

Juvenilia

I am a child in the lunchroom
which is the sometimes gym
singing my known truths: *I love milk*

to which Tanya says *If you love it so*
much why don't you marry it?
And that's a fair point, Tanya.

Why don't I marry this milk, why
don't I plan an elaborate ceremony,
choose colors, invite milk's family

and milk's college friends to stay near,
but not with, us? Why don't I start
picking the poems now to be read

as we wed somewhere necessarily
refrigerated? Just like a child
to think it's so easy—that love

is a one-way act or a matter
of decision. We can't love
what we love into loving

us. Tanya, if I could
why would I waste my time
with milk, or with you, you

whom I decidedly do not love?
I'd be out charming
my indifferent grandmothers

into expressions of genuine affection
and jewelry. I'd be deepening
a correspondence with television

and movie star Michael J. Fox
who I imagine chastely kissing
with my full and future lips,

making the sounds
I've seen on the screen.
Tanya, this is the smallest torture

you'll think up for me, perfected
until junior high starts and I
am in honors classes and you

are not—forgive me this, my own
small wounding, but I am
storing these cruelties inside me

like a library dedicated
to one kind of war. I am becoming
a woman who'll do almost anything

to be wanted. Why don't I marry
the milk, Tanya? Ask the milk
what there is in me to love.

Self-Portrait as Erinyes' Dating Profile

Unzip me from this winter, come
unbog what's left of this flesh.

Snakes? Floss for teeth that ring the tongues
turned stone when they cursed my name.

I am fearsome and I do not need
to be saved but that doesn't mean

I'm not waiting for something to happen.
My to-do list is long and names names.

If you think you're the you I'm thinking of,
let that be the first miracle we make together

alive at the same time here on Earth.
Sometimes, you have to invent the body

you'll be happy in. I was born too much
of everything, but now I'm a kind of pin

prized for crucifying wings, fringing cilia
when you grab me and stab the beautiful thing

to keep it from leaving. The peace you feel
as I shine behind glass, the sting

of your finger singing out blood. Every poem I write
ends up the same—I want you then I'll want you

gone. I am trying to tame my humanness
but like a cat it claws back, hunger

the only language it knows, so come,
boat. Be brave. The ocean was the ocean

before you thought to sail it, and still
it thrills at your sloop, the moan you make

when it takes you, loving you to sleep
on the dark night of its floor.

Unmappable

Kansas coos me into its wheat.
Done with direction, I follow the lightning,
God's arrows insisting even the desolate
   can be a destination.

In the black and white of a winter dawn
   a train zippers the wet land
   to a sky clouded with intention.
It looks more like a photograph

than a photograph resembles the moment
it captures, its frame diverting, its filter
slanting truths. Say I make of this a photo—
   what would the evidence show?

That I was in a body here for awhile
and I wanted this to mean something?
     Is this the alibi or the crime?
And who is the jury to receive this—no one

knows I'm here. I loaded the car in Technicolor
and drove east—had done milked the west
of fresh starts—but the time changed
   so I don't know when I am.

Kansas says it does not matter. Time
rolls over its husks and soil like fog, changing
nothing. So much land—
   anybody could be buried out here.

Midlife/Midwest

Our desert house husked musicless, save
for my clock radio, which I'd tune to synth and sax
to muffle my parents' misery, the first animals

I ever knew. Nights quiet until summer
brought thunder and coyotes pushing against
what we thought we could call home.

The air here heaves with wet heat,
the stereo of cicadas
throbbing their tymbals until such want

is the new rhythm my heart funks to.
They leave their old selves everywhere, singing—
fuck me, fuck me, I'll change.

How once I was a streetlight so I wouldn't be alone,
my yellow eye filmed with moth and filth,
until I learned to dim

and let the stars have their way.
Like this tree-strung choir, I don't trust
a silence, even the one I've dressed in blue,

who calls me *love.* You can choose the house
but not what happens inside. When I ask you
to sing to me, I mean any you will do.

Jane Calls to Clytemnestra

Tulips again. Mouthy, ruthless fools. Nevermind
their cloy and puckering—put your ear here.
Hear—such knocking—crow of a knuckle

cawing on some door. Any loosed woman
can crawl, shouldering a groove into a wall
like a black line before what's after. What it means

to stay, to rumor the addled spackling,
to ochre the lines to language, swirled
as if from your own hand. Here—a man walks in

to a barb; now he's yelling with two mouths!
If you are not laughing, all of the wrong things
have happened to you. Or have not happened

yet. Love him, watch him boat away—I've made
the room a map so you will wait for no news.
See the walls of the city he wants. See what he does

for better wind. What came from you
will kill you. Better to let what made it wander,
not braving the storm but the storm itself.

The night is red—the seas now, too.

He'll call it a cure but you know its real name.

You know what you have to do.

After Ever

Everybody's husbands fall in love with me.
It can't be helped, they know
I'd look good turned to sea foam,
the shell of my pink voice
tumbling til lost on the ocean's dark floor.
Once a man at a bar told me
my hair made him hard
so I gave it to him,
borrowed a blade from the bartender
and hacked it off in clumps.
So many colors! Like a sunset
if the sky was made of body parts.
When I was young I was dead
and my job was to wait
for a good man to kiss—you know,
a man who is good but also into kissing
dead girls. So what could I do?
I forgot my name and got good at math.
I built the bridge you are on now
between the thing you want and the thing
you're learning to leave. Strong, no?
It's made entirely out of the sound
of Czech violins tuning
on an October night, winter
announcing its crisp intentions.
Across the water whips a flag
of a country in which I am the only citizen
and so, also, its queen.

My Best Friend's Abuser Takes Her to Court

A private eye serves her papers at work. Outside,
it's all apples and gourds hollowed to haunt. We stab the flesh
                until it grins. Our black wings unfurl and everyone asks

what we are. *Vengeance*, I say. *Justice,* she corrects.
                He wants her to stop writing about the things he did,
different than wanting to have not done them at all.

                We tongue our fangs in whetting,
button up our lady suits. It is not
                possible to forget the face of a man

who's made you the door to his urge.
                We were not children together, so now I braid
her hair. It takes all night, the married strands

                lioning her like the male
whose only job is murder. In court, he says he
                is the unnamed darkness she writes of. The women

around him sob, Electras mourning the man and not
                the sister he slew. He cries, too, heaving
in a gold-buttoned blazer, claiming his only crime

                was loving too much. The hand he raises,
swearing— as if any god
                could help him now.

Mary Silwance

Originally from Egypt, **Mary Silwance** lives in Kansas City and is a mother of three daughters. She has been an English teacher, Farm to School Coordinator, an environmental educator, and a farmhand. Mary provides writing workshops and serves on the editorial team of Kansas City Voices. Mary also explores ecology from an intersection of justice and spirituality in workshops and writing. While her poetry and essays appear in numerous publications, you can find her work, chapbooks, radio and zoom presentations as well as workshop offerings at https://www.marysilwance.com. When not writing, you can find Mary gardening, hiking, or thrifting.

of being

they kettle overhead
scent and see what is there
but keen and dive
only for what is theirs—

they will not rise glorious
like a phoenix
with mythic feathers
to preen

No.
They will thrust
instead into death.
Feast on disease.
Savor clots of rot.
Slurp decay. Make
together
communion
from wreckage.

For this is what a wake is:

release from
malady   injury   frailty
the gravity of time

lovers of bone

they strip
sinew
   muscle
fat
   flesh
to reveal
the sturdy light vessel
of being
as sacrament.

They then glide
wings spread
rising
                    rising
rising

heads thrown back
eyelids closed
caressed by the nearing sun.

what will be

November
has already
made husks of
what once was

I work fast
against nearing dusk
the sky charcoal streaked

releasing stalks from stakes
vines collapse
withered fruit, now tombs
for cutworm, roll away

tired soil soon tucked under
sheets of russet leaves
my beds readied
for hibernation

I pause
cheek on rake
wood worn smooth
and want
my own gestation

deep silence
to swaddle me

stretch womb wide

a season of my own

making from what once

was cells inchoate coalesce

in increments of soil

gathering already

to ripen into

what will

be

Alongside

Palm sized flames pulse
against snow dappled trees.

Leaves
lit
with the same
orange fire
as the sky.

In the new snow
we make tracks
alongside those
that came before
rabbit raccoon deer.

It is here
I slip.
Tumble down
from a dream of you
into the tender gravel
of your voice.

to the diversity professor

I cannot be your

speaker anymore

the guest Other

called upon

to enlighten

students in

joggers and slides

while their eyes

slide off me

to their screens

while I speak.

while I speak:

detail   habitat   nutritional requirements

    vocalizations   mating rituals

topography preferred   rate of extinction noting

    political predators past and present

        then thread heartstring

                        through narrow FOB mishaps

    appearing exotic

but safe.

while I speak:

sip Starbucks and OMG

my flora and fauna

misguess my genetics

because they clutch

selfies

not

selves

Bitter

is a bird
slender foot
tethered to
a long lead.

Roams far
not free.

Returns
instead

ravenous

for
heart meat
still
pulsing.

re/member/ing

to re

member

do I go back to the beginning
and start over
like a song or special handshake
relying on the first note
first gesture to unravel the whole
or can I remember
right where I am

place my finger
in the middle of a word
sentence page book
in the middle of a library
endless with middles
and recall how it started and why

to re
member

as in
put back together
like Humpty-Dumpty
only it's not a child's rhyme
it's my line

as in

to re claim

re pair

re turn

not to Humpty-Dumpty's wall to be

measured or martyred

but to

myself

to re member

how it started and why

to remember

       I need the quiet dark of upturned soil

my shovel's blade, my pen's ink, cutting through

the crusty now for

the fertile backstory of what's to come

Monkey Mind

Slapped Sanuk flips up
three flights worn wooden steps
lavender mat tucked under arm
its shredded tire smell faint
under nag champa fog.
Denied the wedgy in my
Lululemon pants because
Align is their $90 name.

Prayer hands to heart,
do I look serene?
I strive to look arrived
but I crave French fries and
fear vaginal farts.

Other yogis balance on manicured pinkies
glisten. breathe quietly. smile even.

I snort queef sweat.
My mantra—
fuck you fuck you fuck you fuck you
steadies my breath.

Finally Shavasana.
Stretched in corpse pose
inhaling Bon Iver,
I glare at the cloudless sky

trapped in exposed brick
color of raw beef.

our teacher, Gumby,
voice satiny from weekend trainings
instructs us to imagine
our bodies melting into
welcoming earth's warm embrace.

I picture my body where it is.
Goose-pimpled ashy flesh
and hard white bone dissolving
beyond the studio floor
into the tattoo shop beneath
oozing through the street level juice bar
maybe even dripping down to
a stone basement
before I hit dirt.

So much melting
and I am already
unsubstantial.

in *Euphoria*

I see
a boy crack
a skull
with a hammer
like a poached egg

clotty brain scarlets
the carpet

I see
another boy scramble
someone's face
with a baseball bat

the yolks of his eyes
bubble out
of bloody sockets

I see
yet another boy dice
yet another's head
with a jagged
Vodka bottle

nostril molar and eyebrow
pulped into a crimson omelet

In the three seasons
of *Euphoria*

a story that cycles
around a girl
and her friends

never once do
I see

    a girl
    menstruate

That would be
disgusting.

we trail

a fuchsia umbrella—
the museum guide bearing
a beacon for her brood

herded
we are gape-mouthed
in khakis and Keens
slouched in backpacks
sporting water bottles and trail mix
as if dehydration and starvation
is ever imminent for the likes of us

wired
an umbilicus streams
to our ravenous ears
our minds abuzz
with what once was
we scramble to reassemble
the scattered jenga
of Sophomore Western Civ
machinations military and political
multiple choice   country of choice

we marvel
at feats on placards
dutifully read
hero and battle detailed

erections ensconced
in Ionic, Doric and the other one
--architecture to, by and for victors
the gilded throne filigreed
crown alabaster footstool
the table with ivory inlaid
each country waves opulence
like a flag

herded
now outside to sidestep
with our not so keen
seeing the cow or donkey or camel dung
goats or mangy dogs and unairbrushed
UNICEF children in real time
pressing purses and postcards
against our pressed khakis

we trail
through throngs of khaki
skin and grime
inlaid by centuries of
machinations military and political
multiple choice   country of choice
eyes fixed on fuchsia

spoils

since rape
is a weapon
of war

where are
the ROTC posters
dog tags
21-gun salute
veterans' day parade
the Denny's discount
the *thank you for your service*

to downy-haired daughters
and toothless grandmothers
impaled on soldiers' erect rifles

their bodies bloodied
into unmarked wombs
unmarked tombs
for every god and country
unremarked upon
in history books

Marcus Cafagña

Marcus Cafagña is the author of three books of poetry, *The Broken World*, a National Poetry Series selection, *Roman Fever*, and *All the Rage in the Afterlife This Season*, forthcoming in 2023. His poems have also appeared in *Arts & Letters*, *Harvard Review*, *Quarterly West*, *Rattle*, *The Southern Review*, among others. Born in Michigan, he left Pennsylvania for the Ozarks, where he teaches poetry writing at Missouri State University.

The Surveyor

He idles a white station wagon
across our road, flicks his door wide
as a switchblade and steps over dirt,
the way hot air escapes the surface

of the earth, the edge of wetlands
even this rainless spring can't
lift. My wife knows what's
coming: Christmas Tree Village.

She spits out seeds as watermelon
runs between our feet, newspaper's
classified section wet
as dead skin against the porch.

Then swiping her fingers across
her jeans she's gone inside,
screen slapping while I fish
a smoke, shake out the match,

its tiny blue tail curling
in the heat. And sure enough,
the surveyor aims his tripod,
drums clipboard with mechanical

pencil as if he's grown impatient
with the pines, the wild grass,

the standing swamp that was
Lake Lansing. When suddenly

from this dream of backfill, boon
of condos, multicomplex living—
all of it lost for moments
down that sinkhole of mind—

a blackbird screams and before
his work the surveyor pauses
as if he might reconsider, as if
red wings could wake him.

The Way He Breaks

When I separate the blinds today
I watch the dark-haired kid
across the street, shooting baskets
hard with both hands. He's had it
with the Crisis Center. The aluminum
backboard shudders each attempt,
the ball most often rolling the rim
but not dropping through. He's pounded
rubber over cement too many days,
over battered painted foul lines,
dribbled and faked his way between
imaginary defenders. No one there
when he finally makes the shot.
What holds him to this place?
What act of bad luck?
Who might he miss when suddenly he
pauses, frozen in Olympic posture,
focused on the hoop, the missing net,
as if something has just occurred
inside him that makes all of this
some kind of rotten joke? The way
he breaks from that—sprints
into the highest jump
like someone drowning,
pushing his weight
up off the bottom.

The Shoplifting

The butcher, in his blood-stained apron, catches me red-handed.
To the crime of stuffing
a ten-cent bag of potato chips into the unzipped belly of my
jacket, I plead guilty.
The snack-size Lay's falls out. With his meaty forearms,
the butcher drags me, in my sneakers,
by the collar, over a greasy floor back behind the deli counter.
It's 1968,
and yet I'm held prisoner in the last corner market
of an era gone by.
Sitting on an overturned milk crate behind the deli case,
I can't feel the breeze of a rotating fan
turning back and away before reaching my face. Chopping up
cuts of meat with his cleaver,
the butcher tells me I'm lucky I'm so young. He's not calling
the cops. I fight back
tears of relief. The number I give him to call is not my mother's.
Sick with the stench
of rotting pine and newsprint, I want to remember feeling free.
Then, bells chime
over the front door, and I see my father in his tie-dyed t-shirt.
To spite a forehead
creased with worry lines, his dark hair is cut in Beatle bangs.
It comes as no surprise
he was busted for pot in 1948, that he wore the mug shot
of a smuggler's shame
in *The Detroit News*, that his pop whipped him with a belt.

To hear my father humor
the butcher is to know shoplifting is just kid's stuff.
If my father's fixed gaze holds mine,
it's not for the stealing, it's for keeping my cool.
Shouldering his mod medieval pouch, he leads me back
outside to a bucket seat in his Triumph TR4.

Suits

Saturdays my mother disappeared
in the rearview, my father's bumpy Studebaker

transporting us from hushed suburbs
to the crumbling brownstones

of Detroit. And once he had a date
over in Grosse Pointe Woods

with a dark-haired lady lawyer
who wore the best suits.

Only the best. My father spoke of suits
in hushed tones,

himself a connoisseur
of the Salvation Army downtown.

There I learned the price
of bowling balls, porcelain

swans and plates, everything
mismatched. My father's bulk

charged into sports coats I held up like a matador,
double-breasted dinner jackets

cut before Eisenhower,
before Truman.

Still, he flirted with the clerk
about the name stitched over her breast,

spread a three-piece polyester over her
counter like an extinct bird.

Wore it back in the car.
His *only the best* chiming over the blare

of the radio. Not realizing
as even I did then the bad fit,

the short cuff, oblivious under drink
and song to sweat soaking

armpits, the third and fourth button
cocked against his belly,

tiny threads snapping across his back.
I could see the flaw, imagine

her beautiful disappointment,
one nylon leg crossing over the other.

Dogs

After Michael Van Walleghen

Tonight in Michigan
dogs are barking, whining
and barking through walls,

keeping the woman
in 2-B awake, next door
two albino German Shepherds

in cages without food
or water. Dogs that send
the woman back under the fingers

of electrodes and restraint,
white shoes nipping her heels
as she moaned and fought

for balance. If she could
just focus on something else.
The chipped walls, the buckled sill.

Impossible to do more
than swirl paint
around the can, with these dogs

whining and yipping.
The smell heaves against her
until she squeezes the lid back,

stands all her weight so the rim
snaps shut, then returns it
to the closet. Every surface is clean,

magazines stacked, hands
turning clockwise.
And this is a good year to be alive

but not with this colitis,
these dogs howling pain
in her bowels, the bowl

white as their flanks,
their soft, thin ears.
Nothing to worry about

this blood keeping her up late,
these ulcers
gnawing inside her.

the walls bleeding
and the door whining back
on its hinges against dogs.

Modigliani: Venus Naturalis

In one of his Venetian nudes, a woman who is twisting
    her body in opposite directions
clenches her fists as if extending the moment of orgasm;
    I longed for his woman, as a boy
kept her invisible delight like the French postcard that shows
    a nymphet reclining

in an Eastern setting, an opium pipe's silken hose wrapping
    her wrist with strange
perfume. Nudes were always courtesans, surrounded with
    detail: Diana and her forest,
Bathsheba reading a letter, Eve with a view of the garden.
    Until Modigliani taught me

to love the working woman, housemaids and waitresses,
    I did not love the orchid itself.
There is a peach iridescence, a burnt sienna under his thin
    coats of varnish, a hot bath
in which my wife's breasts seem to float, legs and red toenails
    pinwheeling her back

to earth. The way ecstasy leaves her hair disheveled and
    edged with light, her eyes
weighted under the fatigue of observation, she is like other
    Montparnasse characters
he soon will reject, as if she could be possessed by any man,
    or by no man at all.

Something Faithful

I can't imagine the seasons
of ruffles and turtlenecks until she
allowed it to be seen,

my Aunt Eleanor's throat scarred
by the blade of a knife.
But now it's the itch of healing

at family gatherings. In something
low cut the scar is a deep red
valley into which I cannot

look. Still, she's never accused
my cousin of madness or hated
the heroin he tried to kick

with Quaaludes. She only ducks
her chins at times, says
it shows a mother and son

can live separate
lives since a scar is something
faithful, a way her skin

will never give him up.

Brighton Prison

The mess hall sun exposes a yard,
salt and pepper shakers chained to collapsible
tables, where even we denizens
of United Church jump to the whistle
that calls the men down the tunnel for cell count.
In awkward pairs they wobble
past our Christmas charity and tinsel,
the effigies of children's faces
pasted to walls, as if Daddy were a word
a man in here could forget.
Unaccustomed to the light, they sink
to benches before wrapping paper
and age-graded gifts: Teddy Bears,
basketballs, GI Joes. Most can't guess
what their own child wants, like Darnell in shaved dome
and chilled breath. But I hold my nervous chatter
to see him fuss with ribbons and tiny kid
scissors, trying to wrap silver paper
around the splayed arms
of a Black Barbie doll until it's wrinkled
and frayed, tucked in on itself.
The little card he signs *To Sonny, from Coot.*

Red Devils

His roof punched in, retreads spinning,
his Impala stopped dead in its tracks.
Born with one good eye and one leg shorter
than the other, with a thousand buns
at Big Boy to slice and stack,
Hector's life revolves under the plastic effigy
of a burger in a White kid's hand.

Since the crash he's reclined in a trance
with his legs buckled up on the dash,
as if he were home watching a Tejano singer
on the late late show croon the ballad
of a car like his, launched by red devils
and too much Mescal off somebody's bumpy
driveway into a Knievel jump.

A jump that landed on this suburban porch,
bumper and grill thrust through a bay window,
headlights blazing over the furnishings
of a living room, where Mr. and Mrs. Smith
make a flannel knot, terrified and squinting back at him
like they'd never seen a Mexican
saying his Hail Mary's in a lowrider before.

Gloomy Sunday

If the instrument of your beloved's suicide is within
Your reach, get rid of it.
      -Traditional

This was the time of year, this gloomy Sunday
in October when I descended
our basement steps to the bottom of hell
and found my wife hanging
as if the lord mayor
had lured her to the other side.

Don't let me forget that Lansing place,
and wonder who lives there now
and what they make of our cracked foundation.
Let it be clear, but small, through a lens,
my wife's cropped hair, the chairs
so torn with fabric stripped from their arms.

She promised she'd stay in this poor little world
and redeem the diamond ring,
but the ulcers in her colon did not stop
bleeding and the facelift seared her scalp
to the stitches and the manic depression
coiled her throat like a necklace,

burning pearl by pearl. But she could not
avenge the first husband's fist, or the CMT
at Fort Myers who left her in restraints,

hospital gown on backwards.
Or the snapshot pose with her father
on prom night, the secret bristling

between them. Now the dolorous wind
swings branches, sharp-edged and shadowed
with clouds. Now the radio wakes me
from a bathroom floor in Pittsburgh, the clamor
on every station a summons
through evening's wormy pomp—

acid guitar, saraband whirling
under electric globes, the voice of an angel
blown to dust—as if from my wife's
dying breath, the germ I've caught
will self-inflect. Ridiculous thought,
but I'm throwing my extension cords away.

The Other Side

I'm thinking tonight of the morning
Carla phoned from his farm in Michigan

to say he was wearing the lipstick and wig
and sitting alone on the plastic, red chair

I gave him as mementos after my then-wife
had hanged herself. I doubt anyone wants to hear

his poem in praise of the slipknot,
or would see the sound of gunfire

outside my window in Fairmont Park
as a sign to read it. But here is a man

who even dolls himself up to teach literacy
to ex-cons, whose news that day was the glass pipe

he'd quit. And though it hurts to think of Dianne's
silk scarf caressing his unshaven cheeks,

a cornhusker impersonator
modeling my wife's Parisian splendor,

I have to admire the man for washing
her white chenille and hanging it out to dry,

the robe my dear one wore down each steep step
toward a basement beam on the other side.

Daniel Biegelson

Daniel Biegelson is the author of the book of being neighbors (Ricochet Editions) and the chapbook *Only the Borrowed Light* (VERSE). He serves as the Director of the Visiting Writers Series at Northwest Missouri State University, where he also works as an editor for *The Laurel Review*. He holds an MFA from the University of Montana and an MA from the University of Massachusetts-Amherst. He lives near Kansas City with his wife and children.

Neighbors (I)

"History has made us all neighbors"
—Rabbi Abraham Joshua Heschel

Replace I with you. Replace clouds with branches. Exculpate my heart. Replace my heart with another organ. The eyes. With iris aperture. Or. Hear the body with the body. Extinguish the inner ear. Imagine the scrollwork. There are times when assent is impossible. Hear the way the syllables sound. The words ring. Excise the plague of grasshoppers from the crisp fields, the schoolyards, the white lawns. Recall the patch of pin oak leaves against a backdrop of memorial sky. Fingernail the edges and pull. Walk in rubber soles. Refuse leather. Unless to bind the arms. To wrap the forehead in tefillin. You are made in whose image. Replace neighbor with children. Redact silence since silence is impossible. Also a cymbal. See. A symbol. Replace symbol with synapse. Move on to arrive at the synagogue. Because I believe I am angered by the slightest hiss. Imagine a parade drumming around the town square. The brick-and-mortar courthouse with a hint of roman tracery. See the angles. From various angles. Above. Treeward. Though the legs. The limbs. The thrown pink and blue bubblegum scattering under lawn chairs. Scrambling. Redact stained glass. As a child entering to see swastikas spray-painted on the ark. Now again. Plagued. And plagued by continuity. Layer upon layer. Bewildering specificity subsumed by synchronicity. A ritual. We chronicle. Replace message with memory with message. We feel the past lifted upon us. Differently then. Now again. I am rage but plagued by a hibernating guilt. A cryogenic wood frog. I told myself. This is a safe place. Saved by people. Which people. I had children. I have children. I am afraid of revelation. I am until the sun shines. Once I tried to set aside you. Try again. Once I tried to set aside rage. I keep finding myself driving down the highway confusing blown tires with black crows. They've have been circling for eternity. Do you believe in eternity. Infinity. Affinity. For once. Can we pray without ropes around the prayer. Exchange branches for wires. Extinguish the clouds. We are the murmuration turning over the earth with our predatory eyes. We are the field turned over and under. We want to preserve our singularity. We can no longer look at each other.

The New Light

The sign written in a sharpie says *Be Right Back*
and through the window the light is spilling
or flooding or creeping from the backroom
in the café on Green Street where I'm hungry
again. Today, I am obsessed with addition,
not so much form. Listen, why is the angel
of death so easily confused. I was born yesterday
and the day before and the day before. I read
about a study in the *Star-Ledger* with a cup
of coffee, a brie and arugula sandwich
on French bread that put some old habits
in a new light. If I love popcorn, must I love
oblivion. I'm having a child, must I grow serious.
My grandmother's dementia colluded with cataract
to close the door of words. I'm writing about
something resembling wisdom. Why is safety
still a privilege. Who is the we that dreams of husks
of burned out buses. Who is the we drinking lead
laden water. Who is the we that inscribes or enshrines
the dusk. Which we slowly rolls their rusted
dodge pick up behind me for a block as I walk
after services and then screeches past with tires
burning. Bumper stickers clarifying the air
of suspicion. What sort of reader are you. Am I.

I make birdhouses. I digress. I look like my father
and my mother and the waiter from tomorrow
if tomorrow ever darts inward. The apples in
the basket next to the muffins on the glass counter
have the look of something looked at or looked over
or the sheen of something else. *Terrible. Terrible* says
the bald owner with a white apron and blue plaid shirt
in the corner as he turns off the endless news. I've been passing.
Fearful. Cycling different *yous* to the surfaces. Once
I was invited over to an apartment where confederate flags
and torn pages of swimsuit models holding AK-47s
and strapped with combat knives hid the walls and no one
seemed to notice that I was made of ash. I stood.
I stand in my body. How can I pass on what I bury.
It is impossible to forget the names of flowers after talking
with the florist next door. You would think the weeds
would be different, but they have names—yarrow,
clover, thistle, buttercup, ragwort—and someone
in every language knows them all. I've succeeded
in distracting myself from myself. Have you come
with me. Where the night flutters. I have waited
too long weighing a bouquet—birds of paradise
against roses and baby's breath. Why not a spray
of Queen Anne's lace. It is snowing again.
And I am afraid I have lived too long inside myself
to be to anyone. It is snowing again. And I am afraid
of the kingdom of ends. You see additions
upon stammering additions. I feel guilty for making
love with you. Listen, this is too personal
to be a confession. Apologies gather wherever socks

go when they go seeking their mates. It's a particular
and universal dilemma like the way our legs knock
and piston as we use our opposable toes to free
our feet. This is silly and serious. My son now.
My daughter now—there is a fire in the house,
in the house of annuals, the house of memory, the house
that houses nations. Are we trapped in the trappings
of metaphor. The house of perennials is already
an umber field and we are not born into a cloud
of knowing or unknowing. It is a problem
of simultaneity—and & and & and. We must be
born with this third thing about us or in us
or elsewhere—a grain of an unheard echo. A seed. No,
that's not quite right. We don't really speak anymore
of what it means to be human. As if we were dying.
We speak of clothes and their cast. Of cars and rigs
mangling people. Of grievance and violence. Shuttering
or drifting toward a mass extinction. Can we convince
ourselves that we are real. Is this need. The passed down
Kiddush cup is a pocket watch is a daguerreotype is a trope
in a poem that says Be right back when 'love is what we mean'

We Move in Abundance

It's a ridiculous argument, but my son stands his ground.
Why can't he attach a balloon to a teacup and fly to New
Jersey. Why is our neighbor's yard filled with dandelions
and drift. Why do you own a house and not a home. Why
do you mow the lawn and despiseclover. It's bedtime.
The fawn is speckled. Tears the grass up. So the roots
dangle. From the mouth. Does the gardenia sleep in a
garden bed. Go to sleep. With stars. My G-d. Go to sleep.

And what about the column of air above. The water rights
below. Why is the ground so hard even after rain. Why
do I keep falling in love with words when words mean
less. Petrichor. Petrichor. Bless my children. :דְּססְדְּלב:
What have years done to this poem. Catastrophe upon
catastrophe. Each to each. As layers of sediment disparately
touch. Why is a bell ringing. Why do we long for a past we
never lived or even visited like tourists in Neil Young
t-shirts staring into an Icelandic volcano. Why does my
friend solder stained glass windows in his garage at night
Fumbling with light. Why a bell ringing. Why do I assume
all the hives of my life exist somewhere still as if I could
walk into any one again and end somehow here. Why do
I feel guilty. For writing this poem. The privilege. What
marks us. Helps us. Makes us legible. Think other of us.

Someone is playing a violin on the subway platform again.
Someone has an open case of cast coins and a few fisted
dollars. Someone has a litter of roses. Someone is holding
hands with someone. Someone in white kicks tips upright

on their toes to see the light pouring out from the tunnel. Someone's headphones look like earmuffs. Someone is playing with a bow, gracefully easing along strings, when the shooting begins again and people we know and don't know scream and crouch, scatter and dive, cover heads and fall.

Do we experience the same violence. From the inside out. The outside in. Save it and store it and feed it to each other. Wildly or gently as poison. At the same table. Over passing conversation. At the same altar. Over passing prayer. Bitter. Brittle. Stone. My G-d. Who is not mine. Or ours. Here. Some of us go on to bend down and tie our laces as torrents of people pour past. Some of us go on to lift up faces from the blue light of our phones and shift stream. Go on to clamber out of dreams. Climb stairs and clatter into the evening air. Float off like balloons. Uniformly distinct. Rendered and unredeemable. Earthly and inhuman.

Notes on the Winter Holidays

Even you are responsible
       to more than you. My daughter likes visiting
the pet store. It's like a zoo she says. She wants
a new calico she can walk with a string. On the way
home she says do we sing poems before we light candles.
'Not to see by but to look at.' On one level,
the mind doesn't impose order. The mind
       doesn't impose order. Order presumes
priority. Good credit score. A forwarding address.
My bills accumulate in empty spaces.
My subject position won't stand still.
How did we get here. On one level, we are not
casual acquaintances. Imagine we are pressed
upon one another. For a while we lived
on the second story above The Leader Store
just down the street from The Woolworth,
which still had a griddle and a soda fountain
and smelled of melted butter. I am not nostalgic.
No need. I can still remember the photographs.
I am a frame. Sometimes a window enclosing
and disclosing. Morning comes on in little bites.
We take the subway to the museum exchanging yous
through the tunnel and into the terminal. Imagine
we are pressed against each other. 'Mingled breath
and smell so close.' The silver doors. A cell membrane.
You are a witness only to what you admit. Some words
emit so many possibilities they threaten to burst.

What is light. What is rain. Now a metaphor.
Take two and answer in the morning. We look
and do more than look. My daughter says
you talk with your eyes off. Why should everything
we see interact with light. I am counting
clouds destined for Florida. I moved the store
here. This is inescapably common. Where
is here. Will you pray with me. Pray with your feet
on the pavement. When she was born we didn't know
if she would ever walk. Now she says *my whole body
is a winter storm* as she leaps across the couch upending
the cushions. No digging out. The self is a reintegration
of exponential apologies—a crowd of people
in multi-colored coats, holding handmade signs
and choosing to sit or stand in the same world.
After you. No, I insist. After you.

And the Frogs and Toads All Sang
Because Singing was Earthly

My son and daughter have many aliases. *Stop pretending* argues Frog to Toad. Hop faster. Or you will be eaten. One little leg at a time. Says the addendum at the bottom of the instruction manual in your head on how to build a house out of toothpicks and dixie cups. Why do we need a tiding of magpies. Who calls for a shibboleth. Calls forth. Why do we circle our hands over the cold green ground. Why do we hope to summon a screen of mist. Here we chatter on. Long after. Even inside Badger's belly. We light a candle and set out a picnic. Your end is pending. No, impending. At some point, it seems I've come to believe the seams matter. Frog gives a chocolate chip cookie to Snake who had been laughing criminally all week about animals in swimsuits. Maybe all gifts are down payments on the need for future forgiveness. Toad wears a cerulean dress with tulle, steals marbles from Frog and says, Blah. This morning I held Toad over my head and said *You look like a gumdrop*. Toad said *No, you look like a raindrop*, which is infinitely more accurate. I'm infinitely elsewhere. The grindstone is the millstone of progress. Death is simply a shadow that asks does this make me look fat. In the meanwhile, Toad throws a handful of legos into the air. See slippage and hegemony in the dictionary. Maybe somewhere around a bend or upon a chestnut tree stump Toad and Frog will meet a gecko named Gramsci who will draw a line in the dust. As for me, I keep thinking about 'bananas ripe and green' in NYC windows. The way we take in the little reflections. The way they reappear to shine out of unexpected places. Like later when Frog says *Grandpa is no longer on our planet*. Like later after all the screeching and transnational trade and canal building, Toad will sit next to Frog while the woods sing and gently place her hand on his hand. It will be as breathing. The fireflies seemingly suspended in the understory. *Look,* Frog said Toad *You are falling from the sky.* The legos hop as they hit the carpet, which is what gravity already narrated for us in the interstices. This is about the moment in the story where the RMS Titanic hits the iceberg but the fiddlers are foxes because of alliteration and Archimedes is an old owl friend who speaks of buoyancy. I'm tired of being an iceberg. Or now by implication in another iteration a plague. Tell us. 'We have heard the music.' The mermaids. Tell us. Let my people go. All people. Then Frog says *Everyone still on this planet is a penguin.* And here. Just before the final turn. For a moment. I believed.

from (ד) :: What Have I to Say in My Wrong
Tongue of What Will Come

It's been a long time. My five-year old son says
it's been an evening of accidents
as another toy train derails
or my daughter kicks up the wooden tracks as she darts
to answer   the doorbell.   In moments you imagine
becoming unmoored   you wish   we could pass on
the wind   we suppose to praise
for its song   its voiceless voice   soughing
or convey the spring leaves   caught
            in unwinding revelry.   The morning reveille.
A monad. In '1.08 ± 0.14 billion years.' What sounds
                  in the wooden chattering.
      The branch lines clattering. Is there
'a steady storm
of correspondences.'   What echoes.
Will echo. Echoes in the clapping.

//

Yesterday   and when was yesterday   or which yesterday
in sweltering heat   the clink and clang of a muffler
dragging along   the street brought   attention   beyond
'to bear'   upon   my neighbor's three-year-old child
wandering the middle   median   shoeless and eating
purple echinacea petals as vehicles
motored up and down the road. What have I learned.
Urgently. Sparks bursting. Hovering.
Bounding. Dimming. In all seriousness.
Do we crave the reckoning we crave. Drifting
toward oneness. Obligation. The vague trees
          flee from us and return. As I hurl myself
down the stairs. When the wind dies.
Even when I know the names. I am
your great doorway. Now. Can we.
Now. Hold hands. Now. Look both ways. Now. Cross
          the street. As if over river bottom. Wait together
on the old limestone stoop as the gray lid
          of nimbostratus clouds
begins to close and seal out the sun.

from (ה) :: What Good Are Soft Syllables
When Crows Sleep Like the Dead

'Does the daylight astonish.' Does the orange. Does the navel.

  The chromosome. The absence of silence. Who asks.

Who asks for wonder. May I. Please. Permit me

to open my chipped beak. To sing. To signal. To send

sugar through to the suffering. A pair

  of raptors seemingly confront

a parapet of smaller sparrows

  all perched on the limb of a ghost tree.

A trick of light. Elusive needles. The color of bone. Barely

  discernible in the shift of morning

sun as the roots of each tree

tangle and reach out to one other.

//

On the precipice of losing the light. The sparrows.

       The chicken hawks. The american crows. But at times

I think 'Let all who are hungry

       come and eat.' Not simply. Locusts.

We bundle tightly—how else—against the burning cold. We wear

       our thoughts. Our speech. Our actions. A body

consists of its being. Plus time. In time. I have lost the sense

       that I am one with my skin. So. Compelled. We must

do. Then understand.   Who ripped whom from their hinges.

       So. I critique myself on graph paper

and singe/sign myself an encaustic

       and what I own you will own. So we are we.

          Gently. With glitches. The 'owners

of a 21st century mind'

of mirrors and confection. Mixed and allotted metaphors.

Brainiac and mysterio. Confetti

of canopied light. And all around our 'companions

       are falling' without wings

thinking you do not see

the roots of our design. The materials. Or our desire.

from (ˆ) :: Sand   Soda Ash   Limestone

Imagine you are a seed. Little word. Little one. With iris eyes.
Imagine 'all the trees of the field / clapping their hands.'
       Imagine a perpetual present. A perpetual wind.
The sky now threatening
like a question that cuts to the quick.
Reined. Then. Bent back   the spring
trees iridescent   daylight   at a time of day
spun out   through   the emboldened leaves
clouds strung overhead   dark together drift   as into a closet.
       Do you want me to specify. Should I. 'Trust
to the genius of trees.' I was advised to count.
You had ten fingers and ten toes. Luck. Or. Blessing. Still.
Frustrated. My work never feels to widen. Never closes.
And yet. You revise me. Little word. Surely as I am
       altered in kind. In the speech   you make possible.

Andrés Rodríguez

Andrés Rodríguez was born in Kansas City in 1955. He attended the University of Iowa, Stanford, and the University of California. Upon earning his PhD in Literature, he began teaching at numerous colleges and universities. His poetry collections are *Night Song* (Tia Chucha Press) and *Portal of Dreams* (Woodley Press). He is the author of a scholarly work, *Book of the Heart: The Poetics, Letters, and Life of John Keats* (Lindisfarne Press). His poems have appeared in *Bilingual Review, The Cortland Review, Drunken Boat, Harvard Review, Hubbub, New York Quarterly, Palabra,* and *Valparaiso Review,* among others. His essays have been published in *Sagetrieb, Hispanic Culture Review, Puentes,* and *Lucero.* Several anthologies have also included his work, such as *Currents from the Dancing River* (Harcourt Brace), *Dream of a Word* (Tia Chucha Press), *New Chicano/Chicana Writing* (University of Arizona Press), and *Wild Song* (University of Georgia Press). In 2007, Rodríguez won the Maureen Egan Writers Exchange Award in Poetry sponsored by Poets & Writers. He has twice been nominated for a Pushcart Prize. He lives in Kansas City, Missouri.

Cicadas

Louder now, they weave their song
among the trees, grappled onto branches
where wind never upends them,
where summer strikes fire into a voice.
Like old pipers wheezing the same
crazed note between catches of breath,
they sit in their unreachable height
and drone that underground music
after seven or seventeen years,
raucous lords of the air and earth.

How do they sleep so long in darkness
beneath the surface noise of the earth?
How do they know it's time to rise up
in the hottest month of the year?
What do they see after those murky years
with tiny eyes like beads of blood?
It must be memory's old bright place,
the first desert, prairie, swamp, or wood,
where their cries came bubbling up
to terrify or tire creation's other forms.

A man on my block who worked nights
once shotgunned the trees outside his house
as if that would stop the buggy music.
But as the smoke cleared, it arose at once,
and that man fell back silent, nameless,

drained by those agonizers of throatless song.
When I lie sleepless in my room, unable
to dream or breathe the pressured air,
the sound in my ears pierces my heart
with dusty white pincers, unkillable.

As a boy I'd see one fall from the sky,
wrapped with a hornet in a death-embrace.
They'd land in a blur on sidewalk or grass
and a prolonged shriek let loose—
not like any laugh or cry I'd ever heard,
but still a screeching or beseeching
that arced the air with a zinc flash
whose cinders fell on everything.
I'd watch the brief struggle until
death arose with a king in his arms.

The sudden chill felt back then
comes now with a buzz heard in
chicharras, whose slangy meaning
is electric cattle prods. Somewhere
a torturer enters a cell or brightly lit room
with one of these ravagers of burning steel.
Its blackened head sparks and crackles,
searing the genitals of a woman or man
whose suffering feeds the lords of death,
whose terror lasts a thousand thousand years.

Everything is Dark

Here in Nogales everything totters.
Cardboard shanties spill down the hills
like dinghies listing in a frozen wave.
In the avenue traffic, a peddler hawks
cheap gold watches on both arms
up to elbows. Cars brake,
tires squeal, and our ears can't mute
the blaring district music,
a Mexicoland where you never get lost.

We go like spies among the tourists,
browsing the vendors whose smiles
flay us because we don't buy.
Then I see the *traje* inside a doorway.
She nurses a baby and watches the street.
A toddler beside her pats the tiled floor
with both hands. As we approach,
she stretches out an open palm:
¡Para los niños! ¡Para los niños!

I'm ripped from this moment,
pitched toward another, underground,
where her twin, in a faded *sari,*
sitting on the Paris subway floor,
cries in French for the infant
whose reedy head sags at her breast.
An outstretched skinny fist balls her words.

169

I feel the greasy whoosh of subway cars
before I hear the screech of tracks

echoing off tiled walls farther below.
The longer I stare, the more her words
bleed into footsteps, car horns, Mariachi rant—
a storm of sounds falling world to world.
Then I see that shadowed face and empty
hand fluttering like a flower between us.
The air grows dark. Under my feet
the pavement is mold black. I walk away.
The beggars, hucksters, and shanty sleepers

send up a cry that balls its fist tighter every day.
I look back, feeling her words.
The hand withdraws from sun to shade,
a tiny drop into broken city sounds
that box her in there looking out
through quiet bitter eyes. I lose her
in the setting light that floods brick, glass,
steel shutters, and the few straggly trees,
then closes round us like a mouth.

Something That Remains

They found it one day while
sifting the rubble, months after
the roars faded into desperate
then resolute digging, men
and machines wheezing, still
scrabbling up and down debris.
A backhoe had emptied its load,
a curtain of dust before their eyes,
when it fell a certain way, different
than the weight of dirt, rock,
or molten glass. It dropped
like one short breath held and spent,
observed by those standing close
who'd already seen what the
roped-off onlookers never saw—
a string of nightmares they lived into.
And yet they stood silent when it
blurred the air and fell at their feet,
its hot glow gone dark within
the pyramid hush of earth.
They stepped forward to see
as the backhoe's engine choked off
and a final flight of smoke trembled up.
It was charred, clearly cracked,
but still that organ of feel and sense,
pump and core of the body's light,
child of Venus, divine need, now

a burnt-out root rolling to a stop.
They all stared, the silent lump of woe
siphoning blood from their hearts.
And in that hushed air they heard
the prayer of flesh to be made ghostly.
Then the subway rumbling. Then nothing.

North

This far north, I don't expect to see them
weaving through Manhattan traffic,
darkness and snow descending.
But the sight of these delivery boys
on old bikes, pizzas balanced on a knee,
is a passage in passage. They show me
how generations repeat their pattern
of unchanged changing migrations
from Puebla, Michoacán, Chiapas,
and jungles farther south, always seeking
havens that need but don't value them.
It's all here this far north: the young
future grandfathers, and me the old
grandson watching them glide along
Park Avenue and squeegee clouds
from manholes steaming around their heads.
Even the ghost of my father is here,
standing dumbstruck on a transport deck
bound for war, the Statue of Liberty
a stark miniature goddess watching
as iron waves close between them.
All here and claiming me.

This far north, I hear the Atlantic
traverse its shores, the night's ejaculations
within dark veils, the switch of chains,
and voices so close murmuring
in the tone of overheard captives,
in the cipher of people on the run.

They come and go like windborne
wings under stars. Few ever see them.
Fewer still speak to them, only offer a tip
the way a breeze lifts a bird before wings
chop the air again, nervous soul crossing
the solid wall of money that scrapes the sky.
Met Life. Aetna. Bank of America.
This far north, stuck to the underside
of our existence, these boys lace the streets,
a flurry of deliveries through Midtown,
and even this recalls workers in the fields
bringing food to America's tables.
The past does not pass, and hunger
seeks more than earth provides—
a home in the far places they dreamed up.

I walk north to Bryant Park,
where the statue of Benito Juárez
punches the air with a shiny bronze fist
to throw a light on the street for his brothers
who slip the nets of the city nightly,
changing from wheels to wings and back again.
Now, in the oncoming headlights,
snow smithereened across the raw air,
encrusting heads, arms, and legs,
they emerge from the dark underside
into the running course of the streets,
lit up households waiting for them,
the past and future in their eyes,
migrants to dreams of life, a life pursued,
under the gun, but always on the job.

Mystic Jukebox

I can't not hear your music
that's always blowing rifts,
choruses, looping rhymes—
all the self-encoded songs
that tighten like bands
around the soul's small dance.

You weren't hatched, you wiggler,
you demon, you shadow-god
deaf to all but your own
machinery of unbroken song.
You were annealed by a searing fear
of forgetting everything.

I used to stare at frozen creeks,
absorbed by clarities of sleeping silt
and the dreamless life beneath,
curled into icy crypts.
Oh, I could kill you, grind you
under heel, salt you like a slug,
but I'd melt in the earth as well.

Then *she* came and poured
a new song into my blood,
and the music listened back,
bringing clear-headedness,
a sleeping potion night,
the crystal personality
of a new bell ringing my fate.

This thread of sound leads
deep into a perfect clearing,
where a cool pool cures,
where ear and music kiss.
No more raging or helpless
weeping. I dive into myself,
tunnel and spiral down
to a place that echoes
what I most want to hear.

The Nets by David Caspar Friedrich

There's no meaning in the coarse nets
　　　　spread on misshapen staves to dry;
but the painter stood rapt in their presence,
　　　　watching clouds take up half the sky.
Spellbound birds with wings outstretched
　　　　are reaching, unreaching a hidden moon;
the world in sumptuous night is drenched,
　　　　as waves glisten and puddles swoon.
The eye receives but the heart pours forth,
　　　　and music wells silent in the mind;
stars and wishes fall bloodless to earth,
　　　　caught by arms woven strong and blind.
Past storm and foam and fear they hold,
　　　　sentries by night, fishers in the dawn's gold.

Real Monsters

October 31

Each year I pray they come,
adults and kids together
drifting down the stairs,
leaking through a door
like fat aromas,
or rising from my lungs
to hover over the altar light,
food and photos glinting with
candle-smoke forms.
I see them in the conehead candies,
the shine of *sopa* and Dos *Equis*.
My dead look out from
black and sterling frames,
between us a long night-journey
across deserts, waters,
lambent stars in tortuous clouds.
I've no doubt they see me,
but how? Do they bless or burn?
Do they want to fuse into one
so that I lose all memories
in a flooded grave?

The doorbell rings:
pirates and green-skin ghouls,
Cinderellas and good fairies.
Under all that transfiguration,

tinny voices answering my question
"Who are you *really?*"
Moms or dads wait by the curb,
watching their greatest treasure
as moonlight calls to boys and girls
running door to door, long lives ahead,
until family histories reawaken
the real monsters that spook us,
scatter us under full moons ascending,
night-fliers whizzing past dusk to dawn.
Tonight, anything can happen.
Cities burn to hiphop shouts,
a comet grazes the stratosphere,
some visitor shakes free, some
revenant, lost or terrorizing,
falls and fevers us, possesses us,
speaking of what's to come
as something past,
the uncontrollable god of blood.

Nighthawks

They sounded like nothing I'd ever heard,
so I never raised my head, convinced
one skyward glance would be enough
to harrow me back to a seed.

I didn't know they were wings,
twin worlds of doubt and dreams
that climbed the darkening summer air
to feed on mobs of wiry things.

Once, in the park, I saw them
above our floodlit monument to war,
a ring of white under each wing
like a fat zero or wailing O.

Then I remembered talons
raking my flesh, a faceless stranger
folding me into a hole. Those wings
that skimmed each other crosscutting the air

hovered at the light's molecular edge
and woke me to my nightmares
as one of them paused, plunged,
and made a *wooom* in the night.

I knew it was that voice of sorcery
absorbing me as I enter dreams—

a voice that needed my fear
to have its own body and storm the world.

At school, the voice sucked in
our breath, our days and hours.
It sent us diving under desks or down
slippery steps to a cavernous boiler room . . .

Cuban missiles, the president dead,
black people shot by cops
as cities somewhere burned.
In that stifling dark, they made us

kneel and pray, eyes shut against
the storm outside. I prayed
to not hear that rippling sound
jetting toward my heart.

I look up now years later at night
to see a silent gliding shadow,
huge and solid against millions
of blown suns, and no one watching

this hour but me and the fighter jet
which chases that mute raptor
winging through airspace
and disappearing like a footstep on a wave.

Cat in the Rain

In a cold, early autumn rain I saw
a wisp of blackfur pawing the trash.
I shooed him off, then was sorry,
for with every movement he collapsed
like a drunk running in fast-forward speed.
      A second time
I saw him in the backyard. It rained harder.
From my windowsill I watched him curl
into a sodden ball that would never
roll or rise into the air, there
below my mother's rosebush that
haloed him with pearls. Then I saw
or thought I saw that leopard of my dreams,
black psychopomp, god of maternal
re-immersion, but transformed, torn,
ripped from the skin of a dream.
      Later
I saw his whiskers were snipped off, and worse,
he'd been whacked on the head by some
brutish hand, brain damaged—
the cerebellum, "the little brain"
that lets us walk or jump for joy without
so much as a whisker's breadth of thought,
turned to mush. This cat walked woozy
with the effort of trying to go straight,
stumbling, falling into the lawn,
trembling like someone with Parkinson's

when he tried, tried and failed to pounce.
As he struggled to right himself,
I wondered what electric fury was
stalled, stymied, blocked inside his skin.
I wondered if he stormed or wailed within
at failing his catness, and if he
recalled not only the blows received
but every graceful step that once kissed earth.
          One night
I woke and looked through the window
barraged by rain whose deafening force
was unforgiving. I went outside,
approached the cold, crimped roses to see.
He bolted, a plashing escape across
the watery dark. For two days he came
and went through a hole in the fence,
nestling below the rosebush, my fraught
sorrow's emblem, as if he was giving
himself up to drown in the drumming grass
that would take him like a mother who
washes away the mud of cruelty,
caressing to sinew and bone, white-clean.
          On the third day
I set out a box, bowls of food and water.
Then as I refilled the empties, he crept
out from his cardboard crib, and there,
in the dark surround, two gold eyes stared
on every side. Then he looked up to see
and to be seen. I thought he'd bolt again;
he fell at my feet, but not purring.

No soft, rich voice, only gazing
from solitude, hypervigilance.
And in those eyes the dawns and nights
falling on his searching, the streets
and empty lots hiding him as he
wandered, slept, and woke under the breath
of roses. It all tracked across my eyes.
I lifted him, held his beaten body
against mine, then ran inside the house
to tend the little god who ate and sat
on the windowsill all day watching
the gray wall of rain.

Letter from Midtown

Taped to the window of a public storage building

Looking for the girl
who stood in line with me
7-Eleven last April
Main & Armour.
We talked about snow
high as stop signs
and blowing this town
December in Orlando.
Sat together
in the parking lot.
Twinkies beer & smokes.
Remember?
Forgot your name
sounded like *hay-dee*.
I see with my ears
and they work slow.
Been gone six months
home in South Dakota
nothing but snow
rusted cars & no job.
The oil rigs silos Kmarts
all different now
ghosts on the headlands.
Only your laugh
coming on the air
500 miles away

day after day

runs thru me.

Left two weeks ago

burned my tracks.

Hoping to meet again.

Ready for ocean

a bed on the beach.

If you see this

look for me in

coin laundries

Mickey Ds

bus shelters

tunnels where I sleep

my car dead on I-29

tagged & towed by now.

I'm here and there

Jon Buffalo

a bit thinner.

Leave reply.

This project was made possible, in part, by generous support from the Osage Arts Community.

Osage Arts Community provides temporary time, space and support for the creation of new artistic works in a retreat format, serving creative people of all kinds — visual artists, composers, poets, fiction and nonfiction writers. Located on a 152-acre farm in an isolated rural mountainside setting in Central Missouri and bordered by ¾ of a mile of the Gasconade River, OAC provides residencies to those working alone, as well as welcoming collaborative teams, offering living space and workspace in a country environment to emerging and mid-career artists. For more information, visit us at www.osageac.org

Osage Arts Community